PRAISE FOR

THE EXPERT AUTHORITY EFFECT™ PUBLISHING METHOD

"Hi everyone, my name is William Benner. I'm president and CTO of Pangolin Laser Systems. I met Mario and was very impressed with him. No matter where you meet Mario, you know, he's the best-dressed guy in the entire place. Mario really helped me to get this book out there. And it has been a great success. It has established me as the Expert Authority in laser scanners. I can't make a higher recommendation for me than to work with Mario Fachini. He has been great for me, and right now, I won't work with anybody else except for Mario."

- Bill Benner | President & CTO of Pangolin Laser Systems

"I have a TV show. It's a known fact that on TV, we have to perform on dollars per minute, and it's several thousand dollars a minute. I could easily make money by going on TV. If I wanted to make money, and that was a reason why the purpose was to make more money publishing books, it'd be stupid for me to write a book that takes you a year to write and publish. It's not a good ROI on your time or your expertise."

- Victoria Wieck | International Jewelry Expert & TV Celebrity

"Hi, my name is Lorie Tensen. I am the published author of 'Taking My Hand Out Of My Pocket' less than four months ago, I started this journey, and I went from having an idea

and the possibility to actually getting my book published in 14 weeks, and I'm so thankful to Mario and IWDNow Marketing for walking with me on this journey, it has been phenomenal, and I really appreciate the support that I've received and just everything has been phenomenal and I thank him very much. Thank you, Mario, thank you, IWDNow Marketing."

~ **Lorie Tensen** | Best Selling Author & Speaker

"Mario Fachini is my publisher & PR guy here, making me do these video's, but this one I'm more than happy to do, So to all of you, there are no words to describe my gratitude and absolute amazement, I cannot thank you enough, for making this dream of mine a reality, and I just want to keep pushing all of you to change your mindset to reach your dreams and become everything you've ever imagined."

~ **Kathryn Ryan** | Best Selling Author & Speaker

"There's no way in the world I would have been able to do this with somebody else. Again, I've attempted it in the past. It didn't serve me. It's a matter of fact; I ended up more frustrated than anything. So, this has been a very seamless process."

~ **Rocio Perez** | Founder of Inventiva Consulting

"If you're looking for an amazing business coach, I highly recommend Mario Fachini."

~ **Adel Wilson** | Founder & CEO of Celebrity Media Group

"I've worked with Mario over the phone and online, and he's been very helpful in getting me where I needed to go with promoting my books."

~ **John Cote** | Author, Speaker & Host of Healthcare Elsewhere

THE
EXPERT AUTHORITY EFFECT™
PUBLISHING METHOD

THE
EXPERT AUTHORITY EFFECT™
PUBLISHING METHOD

---

7 STEPS TO PUBLISH YOUR NONFICTION LEAD
&
PROFIT-GENERATING BUSINESS BOOK IN 8 WEEKS

MARIO FACHINI

2X INTERNATIONAL BEST-SELLING AUTHOR

PUBLISHING
Detroit

THE EXPERT AUTHORITY EFFECT™ PUBLISHING METHOD

7 Steps to Publish Your Nonfiction Lead & Profit-Generating Business Book in 8 Weeks

Published by Expert Authority Effect™ Publishing, an imprint of IWDNow Marketing L.L.C.

For information about permission to reproduce selections from this book, email: Mario@IWDNow.com or call (313) 288-2275

For bulk buy orders, visit our website at: www.EAPublishingMethodBook.com

PUBLISHERS DISCLAIMER

While the publisher and author have used their best efforts in preparing this book, they make no representations or warranties with respect to the accuracy or completeness of the contents of this book. The advice and strategies contained herein may not be suitable for your situation. You should consult with a professional where appropriate. Neither the publisher nor author shall be liable for any loss of profit or any other commercial damages, including but not limited to special, incidental, consequential, or other damages.

eBook ISBN: 978-1-957699-00-4

Paperback ISBN: 978-1-957699-01-1

Hardcover ISBN: 978-1-957699-02-8

Limited Edition Hardcover ISBN: 978-1-957699-03-5

Audiobook ISBN:978-1-957699-04-2

Library of Congress Control Number: 2022901929

10 9 8 7 6 5 4 3 2
2nd Edition, February 2022

There is no way, you would be able to experience this book the way I intended you to, with the flow, formatting, viewing, listening, or feel, physically in your hands without the help of the World Class Expert Authority Effect™ Publishing Team.

From the bottom of my heart, I want to say: "THANK YOU," to each, and every one of you on my team, for helping me make my book a first-class experience for our readers, viewers, listeners, and not leaving it to die on Amazon, as a Kindle only, where most end up, to go and do, just that. But for also elevating the new standard with me, of what our clients can expect, and experience, with their own books, and launches.

Here's to our next decade impacting hundreds of thousands of businesses the world over with our new flagship.

A portion of all sales will be donated to Christian ministries & charitable organizations.

Printed in the United States of America

Dedication

GOD

Thank you for saving me and giving me eternal life, as well as the opportunity to serve and be a blessing to everyone I encounter.

MOM & DAD

Dad, I thank you, love you, and miss you. Mom, I love you, and I'm glad you're here, and I can share my newest book experience with you.

FAMILY & FRIENDS

You motivate me to be the best version of me that I can be so that I can be the biggest blessing to you. Thank You for not only creating opportunities, but sharing in the experience with me.

MY CLIENTS

Thank You for the opportunity to serve and lead you with my strengths and passion. As well as have some fun in the process.

THE EXPERT AUTHORITY EFFECT™ TEAM

There's no way I could do this all on my own, thank you for supporting me, so we can support our clients and make a lasting impact on the world.

DOWNLOAD THE AUDIOBOOK!

READ THIS FIRST

I wanted to make this the best book I could for you, so my team and I went into the studio to professionally record the book, AND filmed the experience!

TO EXPERIENCE BEHIND THE SCENES
ORDER & REGISTER YOUR DOWNLOAD AT:

www.ExpertAuthorityEffect.com/EAPubAudioBonus

Contents

"Either write something worth reading,
or do something worth writing."

~ Benjamin Franklin

Preface

I f there's one thing we know as successful entrepreneurs, it's that; sometimes, we're so focused on serving everyone else, we don't always help ourselves.

Between you and me, I got tired of it. So, I did something about it. Four other books, having helped hundreds of others, hosted hundreds of episodes, interviewing hundreds of authors and experts, nearly a decade later, I made the commitment to helping you in a much bigger and better way.

What's the best way I know how and I tell everyone?

PUBLISH YOUR BUSINESS BOOK ON YOUR CORE EXPERTISE!

So here we are. Welcome to our decade of the *"Roaring Twenties,"* the new me, my new life, and serving you like never before.

It's not new to me, but I can't wait to hear what you learned and is new to you. Let's make a dent in this ball of mud.

I'm smiling ear to ear as I write to you, excited to tell you this book is going to monumentally change your business for the better when you implement my method, and that:

This cobbler now prefers red bottoms.

Prologue

Welcome to the **Expert Authority Effect™ Publishing Method.** I'm excited to walk you through my method and have you published over the next eight weeks. Regardless of the day you start reading this, look at the following Tuesday coming up. It could be as little as 1 day away and less than 24 hours from now, or it may be all the way into next week and closer to 168 hours from now. Whatever the following Tuesday is for you. **MARK YOUR CALENDAR FOR EIGHT TUESDAYS FROM NOW @ 7 a.m. EST,** That's the day of *YOUR Book Launch*!

Grab a pen, drink, and snack as we dive into:

The 7 P's of Profitable Publishing:

- **PURPOSE**
- **POSITION**
- **PLAN**
- **PUBLISH**
- **PUBLICITY**
- **PROFIT**
- **PHILANTHROPY**

~ Mario Fachini

"You can stare at the screen and keep thinking about it, or you can smile and do something about it."

~ Me

DAY 1, WEEK 1

..And that's exactly what I was doing.

I just came up with that three weeks and nineteen hours before I launched the 1st edition for YOU. The reality is the same for your book, just as it is mine:

PURPOSE

Why are you doing it? What's the intent? Who is your reader?
Who's going to benefit from it? What is the benefit they hope to derive from reading your book, and most importantly, did you deliver on that promise of the benefit?

YOU are my reason for this book, and I can't deliver on the promise of telling you the:

"7 Steps to Publish Your Nonfiction Lead & Profit-Generating Business Book in 8 Weeks"

If it's not done, write?

See what I did there?—I already hear **The Expert Authority Effect™ Publishing Team** *tsk-ing me, shaking their heads.*

Don't worry! It'll be better than my others. That was also weighing on me too, because if I had you in my audience, and I was on stage, I'd look you square in the eye, knowing you're an already accomplished entrepreneur with six, seven, and likely eight figures in revenue, and you may already have hundreds and thousands of ecstatic endorsers of you, your product, the awards to show for it, and the testimonials to back it up—*hopefully on video, if not I have an entirely different book that we need to discuss,* and yet I would say:

"YOU STILL HAVE MORE!"

Whether you want to speak, have no desire, already are speaking, or you're in a business that traditionally isn't *"Author/Speaker"* geared, without a business book, you are missing leads and leaving profit on the table. If you ask me, that's not even the worst part.

Your prospects still have a problem that you can solve for them— *in record time, no less.*

While you already have a lot of word of mouth, social media, advertising, and referral partners, if you're reading this and thinking, *"Everyone already knows who I am,"* then you can stop reading. This book is not for you. Plain and simple. Clearly, you're already perfect, at the pinnacle of your life and career, and you don't need any help.

If, however, you are emotionally mature, have some humility, and you're looking for a way to SERVE more people—*while leaving a lasting impact,* in addition to what you're already doing that's working, you're not only going to love what I continue to share, but the way I share it.

The truth is, books aren't hard to write. I did my second book in a day, third one in five days, and this one—*well, it's still chapter one, read to the end, and I promise I'll tell you.* As writers, authors, speakers, entrepreneurs, CEOs, hosts, and servants, we complicate them a lot.

I was staring at the screen thinking of ALL THE STUFF I COULD SAY, so I imagined you sitting across from me. We have some great food, some great drinks, and since I love boating and the water—*we're looking over it right now, and you just told me your vision for the rest of this year, and decade.* You mentioned: finally finishing the book that has been on your heart, knowing once it's done properly, how it will help your prospects make a dramatic shift for the better, but you're wondering:

- **What will it take?**
- **How long will it take?**

- How much of an investment will it take?
- What kind of ROI will it MAKE?

We will answer all these RIGHT NOW, and I will expand on them in the appropriate chapters as you continue to read.

What will it take?

- From my lips to GOD's ears.

HEART

I've cried my eyes out each and every time I do this and started to again when I was typing this phrase earlier, *"Look you in the eye from the stage and tell you."* If you want me to rattle off phrases such as, *"The cover needs to be 6x9, 142 pages is the magic number, and you'll be a New York Times Bestseller, but if it is 145 pages, it will sell only one copy—the one YOU buy."* I respectfully will say that you would be missing the point. You would have a small dictionary of terms, vocabulary, websites, and steps that you're NOT going to follow until the end—*if at all.* You would have ZERO context throughout the process. The moment a molehill of an issue arises, you would get stuck and never finish your book. *Besides, every good publisher worth their salt knows the real secret page count is "149,"* *no more, no less.*

That is not what I want for you at all. I want you to leave a positive legacy for your family and your business. I would like you to stand on the shoulders of the accomplishments you've already achieved, for I know there are many. Now it's time to document your expertise further. Permanently. With a period. In ink.

It will take HEART, without a doubt, and if you don't have that, pushing the buttons to make the details happen honestly won't matter.

That's why Step 1 is PURPOSE. What is yours? Mine is to tell you that most of what you think needs to be perfect won't matter. There are only a few things you need to get *"really right."* Your prospects need your help right now. You have their answer right now.

I Wrote This Book For One Person: YOU!

You take action; you are ambitious. *You are already an accomplished, profitable entrepreneur with a servant's heart.*

- This is not for beginners and amateurs.
- This is not for entrepreneurs who solely want to show off.
- This is not for entrepreneurs who always wanted to write a book—*only for the sake of saying they wrote a book. Do it already.*
- This is not for entrepreneurs who solely want a way to "*hook people*" and "*sell them*" on their junk.
- This is not for entrepreneurs who heard they should, but don't know why.

It is for YOU.

In your heart, you feel it's time, but you're not sure where to start and don't know which type of publishing is best for you. Allow me to break it down for you happily.

TYPES OF PUBLISHING

There are two *major—and I shudder even to say one minor*, but let's say there are 2.5 types of publishing. I will explain each type in detail:

- **Traditional Publishing**
- **Self-Publishing**
- **Hybrid Publishing / Vanity Press**

TRADITIONAL PUBLISHING

In the past, traditional publishing was the perceived pinnacle of what every author would strive for in their career. Depending on who you speak with, it still is.

Whether it was the acceptance and validation of someone "*choosing you*"—*I already know I am Chosen, from God, Ephesians 1:11-12, a far higher source than a traditional publisher*, believing they can sell better than you, or getting to see the "*magic behind the curtain*," the illusion was:

"Traditional Publishing is the best and only way to be legit."

I've found since before I launched my *Expert Authority Effect™ Interviews Show* that there are still people out there who think podcasts, YouTube, and social media are a fad, and terrestrial radio is the only game in town if you're going to be legit. Since launching my show and having many NYT, Wall Street Journal and other bestsellers, a very famous gentleman who has sold 500,000 plus copies of his book, which you'd recognize if I name-dropped it, 100's of authors, many who have multiple books if not a dozen or more, and a specific woman comes to mind when I asked her *"How many books have you published?"* she said *"16,"* *"The first was traditional, the next fifteen were self"* ...she has over 75K+ on her email list, last I knew.

Even with having this behind-the-scenes access perspective, I've often thought about gifting the nay-sayers my SiriusXM subscription with a note that says, *"You know this has been around for more than a decade, right?"*

"You need to get a deal first."

You can't just walk up, agree to play by their rules, and let them take your royalties and profits. They must allow you. If you don't have an agent, you have a slim chance, even if you desire—*and consent.*

Marketing and promotion: I can't tell you how many times I've heard, *"I think they'd be able to sell more books for me."* If you believe someone else can sell you better than YOU can sell you, clearly, you're missing the entrepreneurial spirit, and that's a shame. The reality is traditional publishers expect you to do most—*if not all the marketing and promotion.* That's not their job. Most traditional publishers, if not all, have been around 100 plus years, and they have the networks, but they may not do all the marketing legwork. In the past, when things like cable TV and brick and mortar movie rental stores were the only game in town, using a publisher was your only option.

Amazon changed that...a lot.
Google books changed that...a lot
iBook's changed that...a lot

Audible...shall I keep going?

While I'm at it, if you're modeling a 20-plus-year-old book cover because *"so and so"* did it that way, you're in for a rude awakening.

If you simply copy others without context, you've already lost.

"You need a large following before you even start."

Many successful entrepreneurs have told me—*including one of our concierge-level clients who came to us because he wanted help with the strategy and marketing of his book launch.* He said:
"They [the traditional publishers] told me I need to get my following to at least 20,000 first, before we can even start talking about signing a deal."

If this is you and you want this version of prestige, have at it. traditional publishers have approached me multiple times now, and while I'm confident with my marketing abilities, I know I could fill in all of the gaps they lack. For no other reason than a personal testbed to share with you, I've considered it. However, I can't get past this last one:

TIME AND MONEY

I've asked numerous clients, authors, speakers, friends, colleagues, and VIP guests of my show who have done it and answered this question:

"You need 18-24 months from start to finish."

"YUCK! No, No, thank you, that doesn't work for me. On top of that, the traditional publisher is going to retain ownership, rights and take an additional % of royalties while I lose creative and marketing control?

"Let me guess; they also want to give me a $1,000,000-plus advance, just for consideration."

This scenario reminds me of this great quote:

> *"Experience is learning from your mistakes;*
> *wisdom is learning from other's mistakes."*

> *~ Someone that wasn't me*

The 100% traditional approach is for the following situations:

- If you're already somebody who can get a $1,000,000 advance or more.

- If you already have a large following, if you're too busy training for the Stanley Cup, Superbowl, World Series, the NBA Finals, an Emmy, Grammy, or Golden Globe Awards.

If you go the traditional route, I warn that you likely won't have marketing support, you will lose a lot of control, as well as profits and royalties. You may, however, have a higher chance of getting in bookstores—*if you think more people still walk in a brick-and-mortar store to buy a book than shop from their phone or computer.*

The 100% Traditional Publishing approach is NOT for:

- **You**

- **Me** *(for now)*

- **99% of the entrepreneurs out there**

A caveat for your consideration, you very well could qualify. I know many personally and professionally who have, and do, and perhaps one day I will—*as mentioned for the experience.* Just make sure you're happy with the terms, and even if you are, there will more than likely be aspects that fall outside the scope, and you'll have to incorporate *"a fair amount"* or at least some of what we'll keep covering, especially on the marketing.

SELF-PUBLISHING

If you can do it all, every part of the process, every last thing, with your existing knowledge and expertise in all of the areas, all by your single, solitary self, this approach can work for you.

You may get excited about this, or your blood pressure may just have risen, and your heart skipped a beat.

The upside is you have total freedom and control. The downside is that it's a multi-faceted, multi-layered, multi-step process requiring a myriad of skillsets to do everything at the highest level for everything involved, even if one of the competencies necessary IS in your area of expertise.

Anyone can upload a document to Amazon, but most bookstores will not take any books from self-published authors or anything that came from Kindle Direct Publishing (KDP)—*I will cover why in a later chapter.*

Self-Publishing is for:

Self-publishing is a good option for many people who value their money more than their time and good for them for pursuing it. It's exciting to know that this started becoming an option over a decade ago. It didn't exist in the early 2000s in nearly the capacity that is available now. I encourage everyone to share their expertise, message and make an impact on the world.

Self-Publishing is NOT for:

Most likely, YOU.

You choose to be of a different caliber and to publish your business book professionally; it's going to take time or money. You have the money, but time is something I know you–*and I*–wish we had more of.

Hybrid Publishing/Vanity Press

With the emergence of self-publishing, Amazon, and the new age of the book industry, a new pseudo publisher was born, one that uses smoke and mirrors to make the book advance promises of the traditional publisher, touting the freedom of the self-publisher, but ended up having a worse deal than both. Based on my experience, I present the following warnings:

Watch out for anyone who claims:
"All of the up-sides of self-publishing without the work."

Or something generally similar with different buzzwords.

Let me tell you that there is work involved. It's a simple process, but it's not point-click easy. There is always work involved. It doesn't mean you have to do it all by yourself, but you can't just skip the required steps in the process or take forever to accomplish them.

- **Watch out for anyone that's *"paying an advance"*— *even a small one* AND taking a large chunk of control and royalties.**

- **Watch out for anyone who's making it sound like they invented publishing, printing, or writing.**

I'd love to meet Gutenberg and thank him for the printing press, but the last time I checked, he's not around.

YES, the MEDIUMS have changed, but the core process has always and will be the same. It's not easy. It involves work, but it is simple.

- **Exercise caution when you're getting lumped into a *"book"* with 400 others, and it's going to cost you the same, if not more, as professionally publishing a book on your own would be. While I understand the appeal—*and have even considered it, since I already have multiple books of MY OWN*, if we're still talking about a business book, only one person is making the majority of the profits from that book.**

Unless you're the one publishing it for the other 399 people, it's probably not you. It's nearly impossible to have, and be the authority when you're sharing it with what seems like hundreds of others. *I'm overemphasizing this point, but don't think I haven't seen books with dozens and dozens of others—catch the concept.*

- **Lastly, watch out for anyone who's publishing anyone and everyone under the sun, slapping some stuff together with paper and a cover and calling it a book just to elevate the client's ego so they can get their check.**

At **Expert Authority Effect™ Publishing**, I have and will continue to reject applicants who I sense do not have their prospect's best interest at heart. Just because we can publish your professional, high-quality business book for you doesn't mean we're going to. If you try this even ½ of a %, I assure you I won't do it.

At **Expert Authority Effect™ Publishing,** you keep all the rights, royalties, commissions, and you keep all the profit. That's what we want, that's what we do, and that's why we operate to this standard of excellence.

Choose wisely.

Let's continue to bridge the gap from PURPOSE to PLAN, not only to get inside your ideal readers' hearts and minds but in their offices, homes, and vacations. If you're with me—*regardless of where you physically are*, say, *"It's my time to shine!"*

How long will it take?

Eight weeks. That's easy. I wish I had more to say since I am writing an entire book, but you can ask any of our published authors—*I invite you to check out the testimonials on the website.*

Jotting thoughts down isn't that hard. Getting it on Amazon and online retailers isn't that hard. Telling people about it is not difficult. Knowing your PURPOSE and who your ideal reader is, and how you will serve them through the text is not a challenge. Following **The Expert Authority Effect™ Publishing Method** for irrefutable results, as our authors have, is incredibly rewarding. My goal is to help you feel that, along with many other feelings of accomplishment.

Looking past your flaws, weaknesses, vulnerabilities, deciding the time is now, taking action, keeping the momentum up, and seeing it through isn't always the easiest, as you know, but doable. You've already overcome these things in other avenues. We both know it takes heart and a little more than most are willing to give.

Year after year, I have intentionally refined, tweaked, purged, and enhanced my mission statement to say:

"My goal is to have an extremely high quality, professionally published business book for you in the shortest amount of time, without stopping your life and business to do it, so you can reach your ideal prospect when they become your ideal reader. That is when we can lead with our results, let them do the talking for us, and cut out the nonsense."

The Expert Authority Effect™ Publishing Method is eight weeks at it's core. For a short time, in the early days, it was twelve weeks.

It still worked, but it just felt too long to me. I've done it as quickly as three weeks. My third book, **The Expert Authority Effect™**, was published in five weeks.

I am proud to say it was written in five days while I was organizing, planning, and promoting my VIP book launch event and launching books for other authors simultaneously—*over the 2016 Thanksgiving holiday, and yes, it was all intentionally done to be another inspiring, encouraging, success story for you, the same as this book.*

If you think that's nuts, I encourage you to re-frame. I don't want you saying *"this isn't for me,"* because I wholeheartedly believe every business needs a book, including yours. This goes back to what I said earlier, HEART...*so why the disbelief?* I know this isn't the first time you summited your personal or professional Everest—*perhaps the real thing,* got awarded for it, AND shared the story, so why now? THAT is the cinch point.

You're in good company. Don't dwell on it, but take a minute to look deeper. Honestly, it may be—*it is, some False Evidence Appearing Real.* If you'd like to discuss your specific situation, I'd be happy to help you unpack that.

www.ExpertAuthorityEffect.com/AuthorUnpack

Your prospects also need you to unpack that because it's what's stopping you from serving them at a higher level right now.

"Faith and fear cannot co-exist."
~ Neil L. Andersen

If that excites you, that is fantastic! You're in great company, already on your way to having your book completed, in your ideal reader's hands, and making an impact.

Now...I'm not going to act like we can flip two switches, and everything will be groovy. It is eight weeks for a reason, not eight hours or eight days. One day you might go nonstop, give it your all, leaving it all on the table, but go to bed frustrated, stuck on that *"one thing."*

The next day you wake up, and BAM! Something comes to you, and without a second's hesitation, you know it's the answer you've been searching for. Cool, so we go with that.

You don't need a magic spindle or an abacus to tell you what you've been doing is right or wrong. You need to know:

- **Who am I serving?**
- **What am I serving them?**
- **Title**
- **Sub-Title**
- **Chapters**

I'm smiling because it's really that easy, and as much as I want to lay it all out here, I noticed that the *"Plan"* is two chapters from now. That's where I can go into more detail, but again, since we're having dinner, enjoying the view of the water and there's a cocktail napkin right here, let's do exactly what I did to plan **The Expert Authority Effect™**, and throw the most epic VIP book launch party and awards ceremony for you once it was published.

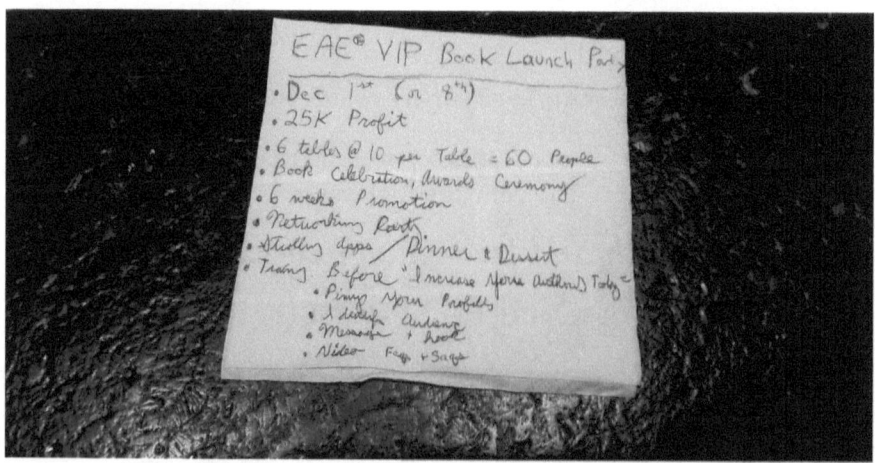

Do you think I'm making this up?

I'm a simple man. I'm not being over the top. When it comes to business, I keep my stress down, my profits high, and I serve with all my ability. I have a lot of fun in the process. I'm not sure if that's my official motto, but if you haven't gathered that about me yet, you will, by the time we reach the end of this book.

What's the Investment? Welcome to Wonderland! The disciplined side of me is curbing the fun side of me, and as much as I'd like to share all the possibilities—*we'll save that for my next movie,* the answer is:

Investment options range between $5,000 and $35,000, with a sweet spot of $15,000-25,000. For going through our process, our concierge clients have invested this amount for a wonderful experience and proven results. Investing with **Expert Authority Effect™ Publishing** is something that you can be proud of knowing you won't have to touch your business book for the first year or longer, at which point, we would be working on your re-launch, or perhaps your second and third—*business assets*—by that I mean, your next books.

Now let's compare a lower and higher investment:

Lower $500 - $4,500
It can be done, but should it? For others, yes, for you, I don't advise it. Even Chris Rock has something to say about it:

> *"You can drive a car with your foot if you want to, but that don't make it a good *** idea."*

> ~ Chris Rock

Higher $40,000-$100,000 plus
You MAY require some special attention, and you're worth it. In most cases, however, you can be a borderline nitpicker or perfectionist. You might be the type to drag your heels. Maybe it's the elephant in the room, or should I say *"ghost?"*

GHOSTWRITING

I loved the show Ghostwriter when I was a kid; I know there are a lot of authors who have done it. I know professional ghostwriters who will be happy to do it for you. I'd be more than happy to make an introduction if you're interested in going this route.

I have nothing against it. However, I haven't done it personally or taught it at 100% of the capacity you may be thinking. Some, however, have compared my method and called it similar to ghostwriting. While it may be, I still don't feel it's enough of the case to claim it—*and still don't think it is, but you're welcome to decide for yourself.* So, I'm not going to speak or write about it, for now, past this.

Here's why:

POSITION(ing) *which I've dedicated for the entirety of Chapter 2.* My entire training, coaching, consulting, speaking, book, brand, and the show is:

The Expert Authority Effect™

At it's core, it's what I've helped hundreds of private clients achieve over the years and have taught to tens of thousands of people. It's not just about *"looking the best"* but *"being the best."* That's why I'm particular about who I even allow in my programs. Even if they qualify, I do not work with someone if they do not embody certain traits that align with my values.

In good conscience,

This next bit may be considered controversial, and to be honest, I even considered redacting it. However, I haven't held anything back in this book, so why start here?

I AM NOT SAYING everyone who ghostwrites does this, not one bit. I, however, just like in business, have come across some in the publishing world who not only *"let it slip by"* but actively promote it.

I can't support having someone else do all of your work, and you are saying it's yours. I think, if done properly, with the right intentions, it has it's place and can make sense for some people, but I specialize in and advise top-level entrepreneurs at a certain level. How terrible would it be to create a book if you're not even sure what's in it and can't even speak on it?—*Remember the "Vanity Press" warnings earlier?* When you hit the stage, it would be a liability instead of an asset for you.

Even worse beyond that, however, to me, it just seems wrong.

WHAT DO YOU VALUE MOST: TIME or MONEY?

Very often, I advise my clients to:

"Cut back to scale up."

~ Mario Fachini

Life has no shortage of ways to steal your time and keep you distracted.

Anything you want, you can have, or do 24/7/365—*which in and of itself, to me, is sad, in most the scenarios. Don't ignore your family & live your life as a commodity.* So then, how do you get it done?

"Cut back to scale up." The problem now is prioritizing. If it's not a priority, it won't get done. Once it IS a priority for you, there's nothing that can be done to stop you from doing it.

PUBLISHING OPPURTUNITY COST

Let's discuss the publishing opportunity cost of your book. To do it properly, you need to make it a priority, at least for eight weeks. I'm giving you my best, don't try to shortcut the shortcut.

There are Three Parts:

- **Business write-off**
- **Dollar to time comparison**
- **ROI**

I'm laying out the streamlined way to accomplish this, where it doesn't have to consume your life and take you 100 to 200 plus hours of your own time.

BUSINESS WRITE OFF

First off, before you decide on any publisher, know that your book is a marketing expense, which—*most likely*, can be a write-off through your company. I'm not an attorney. I do, however, have them as clients, VIP Guests on my show, and I am open to playing one on TV or in a movie. The point is, consult yours first. There is a high chance you are one, so that's good if you decide to go about this on your own, fantastic! I will be happier that your book is out in the world than stuck in your head, and I'm glad the exercises and information in this book helped you. There again—*most likely*, will be some expenses you can write off, but not the total amount, since you're doing it yourself.

DOLLAR TO TIME COMPARISON

Let's look at your income relative to the opportunity cost of finishing your book:

Let's say you make $10 an hour. 100 to 200 plus hours of work is only $1,000 to $2,000. I would suggest you go about this on your own, follow it to a "T," and let me know when you've finished; I'd love to check it out and share it.

Use @MarioFachini and #ExpertAuthorityEffect

If you're more in the ballpark of—*based on a 40-hour work week:*

YEARLY INCOME	HOURLY RATE
$300,000	$144
$600,000	$288
$900,000	$432
$1,200,000	$576
$1,500,000	$721
$1,800,000	$864
$2,100,000	$1,009

Multiply your hourly rate by 100x to 200x plus hours here, and you get:

YEARLY INCOME	REAL COST TO DIY
$300,000	$14,400-$28,800
$600,000	$28,800-$57,600
$900,000	$43,200-$86,400
$1,200,000	$57,600-$115,200
$1,500,000	$72,100-$144,200
$1,800,000	$86,400-$172,800
$2,100,000	$100,900-$201,800

With the straight dollar to time comparison, it's apparent what the highest and best use of your time is.

For the third part, permit me to slide right into your last question.

What kind of ROI will it MAKE?

An additional six to seven figures plus, if you apply my method, and do it right following the process. This may be achieved in short order or over time.

What is a new client worth to me?

Whether your product or service offering is $5,000 to $25,000, or upwards of $100,000, like mine, it will vary based on the service level. That's what makes it even more exciting, let's do some basic math.

Exactly how many additional units do you have to sell to make it your new *"Best Month Ever?"*

Every New Client Is Worth $ _____ To Me *(fill in the blank)*

What about the enhanced speaking opportunities? And the people competing for you to come to their event since you're now an author and speaker, vs. speaker only—*wishing you had a book?* Perhaps you already have a book, but it was done long ago enough that it was a *"different time,"* and you'd like to know how to best leverage it for current and future events.

"PUBLICITY" will be discussed in more detail as you continue to read into Chapter 5, but the benefits of being in the world's largest online bookstore, as well as the other sixty-plus sites, AND having the new opportunity to advertise on the platform with paid traffic means you can crank your marketing up and down at will, to buy more leads for your book, and ultimately your business—*just as one quick example of another new opportunity option.*

How much extra will revenue increase when you can return your focus to serving your prospects instead of being distracted, thinking about writing your book, only to get lost in the process?

I didn't even mention the new asset—*your book, we've created that you get ongoing royalties from.* In addition to straight profit from book sales, when I show you the best way to have them printed on-demand, with the best margins, as well as showing you where you keep the highest profits in the industry, not to mention the options to leverage your expertise beyond the book further, simply because you decided and committed to doing it right by working with **Expert Authority Effect™ Publishing,** it becomes a very exciting prospect, don't you agree?

Each book becomes your new business card. You just expanded it's shelf life from the typical two days to more than two years due to the perceived higher value of your book over the business card. Additionally, how to have your book stand out online and offline, even over other books?

This is just the tip of the iceberg, so I will segue into the next chapter. This last one is also an example of *"Position(ing),"* as well as profit potential—*and yes, it was higher up, I realized it, and moved it down for a smooth transition, let's not over-complicate every step in the process.* If you get nothing else from this book, I hope that by the end, your wheels are spinning faster than Will Smith's Porsche at the end of the original Bad Boys when he says, *"It's either him or us."*

I don't want you only saying, *"That was a good book,"* *"I got a nugget,"* or *"that was nicely written."* While I am committed to making this the best-written business book I've ever done to date. That is one of my goals: to push the envelope from the last highest peak. I'm sure it's also your goal, too.

I will also tell you right now, I'm not going to take a year perfecting it, nor should you. **You should do your best, put your all into it, and GET IT OUT THERE**. While it will mark my new personal best. By the world's standard, it may not be the *"best written,"* but it will be the best selling.

I specialize in business book publishing, because that's who I am, and that's what I care about, and you will see that as you continue reading.

*"Why only read a book,
when you can write one?"*

~ *Mario Fachini*

Position

DAYS 1-3 *(7 MAX)* WEEK 1

This, for the most part, is self-explanatory, you very well have all the authority and positioning in the world, or maybe it's "*VERY GOOD*," and you simply hope to gain some new ideas to enhance it further. Either way, you shouldn't need more than a few days to decide on **where you want your business book to have it's final position in your marketplace.**

All books are not created equal, and here's why.

A book is tangentially nothing more than paper, ink, glue, bound with a cover, most likely either gloss or silk laminate—*but we'll cover that difference in an upcoming chapter.* Nowadays, most consider it to be an electronic file—*but don't get me started on that.*

The words are what matter, and not everyone uses them the same. If the words are different, the book is different.

The Root Word of "*Authority*" is **Author.**

Authority is a position that's not "*Supplicant.*"

Authority is also defined as: "the power to influence others, especially because of one's commanding manner or one's recognized knowledge about something."

Let's now look at the definition of **Expert:** *"a person who has a comprehensive and authoritative knowledge of or skill in a particular area."*

When you combine these together, you have your **Expert Authority Effect™ Positioning.** THIS is where you want your book to be positioned, your content coming from, and your prospects seeing you.

We know that business isn't for everyone, and we know that we

---

don't fit the typical mold. We look for competitive advantages, partners, investors, or we create them. Sometimes this isn't enough. The process can only get refined so much; our teams are already on board; our product and service are the best in it's class. So why are you looking for more? Don't you have it all already?

You know there's more...it's *"Positioning."*

Positioning excites me, and I love sharing it. To an extent, it has nothing to do with *"publishing"* yet has everything to do with it.

Positioning is rooted in storytelling. Storytelling is the greatest marketing tool humanity has ever had, and marketing is the greatest storytelling opportunity humanity created.

Let me further elaborate on this point because it's that much of a game-changer.

If this is your 1st time hearing it, or 100th, my goal is to reinforce the point so that it becomes part of you, and you realize it throughout your entire business from this point forward.

I've said this and taught it for years, but between you and me, I've even expanded this chapter, so it sinks in even further because it's not just business.

Here are just a few areas *"positioning"* plays in your life—*and yes, there's more, and now that I'm mentioning it, you'll realize it easier and see it in nearly all you do.* I would love to hear your real-life experiences from before and after. Who knows, maybe I'll put some of your examples in the next edition of my book.

People, Places, & Things.

PEOPLE:

- **If you don't like someone, they can't do anything right**
- **If you DO like someone, they can't do anything wrong.**

Don't believe me? Let me say this *"Your kids & loved ones."*

You know darn well you can think of someone's kid from some point in your life that CONSTANTLY is misbehaving, lashing out, and generally just acting a fool.

You also know, in most cases, the mom who says things like *"that's so odd she's normally not like this,"* and I bet like me, you have to bite your tongue from saying, *"do you mean when she's sleeping? Because every time we're at the pool, this happens, as a matter of fact, every time she's around anywhere, this happens, so please elaborate what you mean by not normally."*

You may be thinking of someone's son. Generally, boys are the ones jumping all over the place. I'm thinking of people I went to grade school with years ago, and while I won't name him—*even though some of my close friends would be able to guess the girl in the paragraph above.*

This, by the way, is a real-life example. She slapped her a lot. Let me clarify; the young girl slapped her mom across the face when she was within range of tying her shoes, putting on a jacket, generally didn't like what she was being told, etc. The scenario I'm painting is that if you ask the parents...*the kids can do no wrong.*

On the flip side, there are, unfortunately, some other parents who act as if the kids can do no right. This has 1,000% to do with the positioning of the individual and the affinity to the other.

Positioning: Put or arrange (someone or something) in a particular place or way.

Affinity: A spontaneous or natural liking or sympathy for someone or something.

"He loves her so much he puts her on a pedestal."
"She loves being on a pedestal; she can do no wrong."

EMPLOYEES, CONTRACTORS & VENDORS

You've had good ones, and you've had bad ones just like me, some may not have been direct hires by you, and perhaps you never liked them from the start. Conversely, there are others you may keep giving more and more rope, time and time again, and all they seem to do is keep wanting to hang themselves with it, and you don't want that...so you give them some more so they're safe, but it has nothing to do with you.

In either scenario again, what does this do to you, your company, and your brand?

CUSTOMERS VS. CLIENTS

This is almost too easy. Do you want a lot of customers, or do you prefer to serve your clients?

PLACES:

RESTAURANTS: *McDonald's vs. Ruths Chris*

Don't they both specialize in serving meat-based entrees? (*I intentionally left this as "based" and not "focus" for the humor*)

AIRLINES: *Spirit vs. Delta*

Planes are planes, aren't they?

SHOPPING AREAS: *Dollar Stores vs. Premium & Appointment Only Stores*

They both sell stuff; aren't they the same for that reason?
How about the lines at these places? There are usually two main options: the "waste your life away waiting" version or "VIP." You could argue there may be variations, but at the end of the day, you are making a decision overall for one or the other. How about the seating at these places? Same principle at work, different end product. First class vs. economy experience.

COFFEE SHOPS: *Starbucks vs. what seems like everyone else.*

How dare you not spend $7 on a cup of coffee and $5 for a muffin from someone that has an extremely high level of disdain for you, simply because you can actually afford it! Maybe you love them, maybe you hate them, most likely something in between, either way, it's another example in real life that another company plays into and knows 150% what they're doing.

AMUSEMENT PARKS: *Disney.*

I literally can leave it right there, and you'll get it. I could joke, however, and ask, *"Are there really any others?"*
I hope by now you're catching the point as I begin to wrap this up. I would like to think all businesses care, and all people care, and again you can argue *"he or she does or doesn't"* or *"this company does or doesn't,"* I think they all care—*to a point*, some care more about the people, others care about the money, and there are degrees of everything else in between.
Since these following examples are all kind of closely related, I'm going to group them as one:

A SHOW, PARTY, VACATION, OR EVENT, ETC

There are shows at the local grade school and shows on Broadway. There's little Timmy's birthday party and the Met Gala. There's the timeshare presentation *"vacation,"* the Ritz, and the Four Seasons.

I really don't want to say *"one is better than the other,"* even though to most one clearly is, because again, it comes down to how it's positioned.

When I was in high school, I went with a few hundred of my friends in band to march in the Hollywood Thanksgiving Day parade and play at the Hollywood bowl; I loved it! I literally, as I write this, can't tell you where the heck we stayed, but I'm smiling thinking of the—*again literally, hundreds of friends that were with me and nonstop fun we had the entire time.* That was then, now, yeah, the Ritz or Four Seasons sounds more enjoyable, I would, however, still want to surround myself with great people, maybe you're one of them.

THINGS:

CARS:

Cadillac / Mercedes / Maserati / Ferrari / Rolls / Bentley / Lambo VS well... I don't want to put anyone down, but I have 3-5 coming to mind. Feel free to insert yours.

Know this: *"Not all cars are positioned equally."*

PROFESSION: *Neurosurgeon vs. Garbage Man*

I pray I never need a neurosurgeon, but if you are one, kudos on the training, and I'm glad you're around. With that being said, I'm sure you'd agree you're thankful for the sanitation engineers making our everyday lives more enjoyable. Again, two careers with different positioning, both important, but one is generally always positioned higher.

TECHNOLOGY: *Apple vs. Every other PC builder.*

I have both Apple and PC devices. They are tools to me. Each has a purpose, with it's own set of pros and cons. Right now, I'm typing on a PC. A little further down, I wrote from my Galaxy phone.

In other parts, I simply spoke them out. I did, however, preview the cover artwork on my iPhone and Android, as well as multiple other devices. Regardless of what you choose, for whatever reason, it's personal to you.

Big props to Apple for hyper-defining a market segment as a premium product, not only for a campaign or holiday push, but for decades, and continue to do so to this day.

Are they really the best bang for the buck? It depends on who you ask and how that person perceives their positioning.

Whether you're for or against, you can't deny again, another company that has their position in the market nailed down to a science.

MOVIES

A-List celebrities and big-budget movies or B films.

YOUR NAME:

In personal relationships, you're only as good as your word, and your name is only as good as you. Some are born into a great name and don't maintain it. Other's never had it and made one for themselves.

What do people say about you when your name is mentioned?

Do people get excited when you walk in the room or run?

Our reality is the perception we attach to it.

We've both heard for years:

> *"People do business with people they Like, Know & Trust."*

I would like to expand on that and add,

> *"Respect the person and what they do AND believe they can get you, what YOU, want...in the timeframe YOU want, the way YOU want it, and within YOUR budget...or close to YOUR desired end result."*

I'm the best person or company in the world!

You can say it all day, but it doesn't make it true. The truth is if either is not accessible to the person seeking them out, they're not the best solution.

I'm the best person or company in the world!

Again, you can say it all day, but I'll share with you a quote I created, inspired from pitches to be on my show **Expert Authority Effect™ Interviews**:

"It's not that you're not qualified. It's just that I don't like you."

~ Mario Fachini

From my lips to God's ears, they were beyond qualified; I just didn't like them. You also need to know, that's okay! You don't need everyone to like you, your product, or your service.

Companies for years made it feel like they had the golden goose and the prospect needs to sell them on why they should let them buy their product as if to have the prospect say:

"On a scale of 1-10, How much do you trust me?"

Since the advent of computers—*and even more so the internet with online shopping and eCommerce,* I believe the tables have turned, and prospects now ask:

"On a scale of 1-10, How much do I trust YOU?"

Positioning, in a business nutshell, could be easily determined by asking yourself: *"Am I delivering a transactional experience, or transformational?"*

You could also ask yourself: *"Am I currently positioned in a way that's congruent to my core goal and mission?"*

THE NATIONAL ANTHEM

I had the honor and privilege of experiencing this again first-hand the day I wrote the expanded section above.

I'm glad it happened so that I could add the experience to this book. It is a beautiful, inspiring sight to see everyone stopping what they're doing to prioritize the song and moment.

While I could do an entire book and have done an entire training, with marketing psychology insights about how to improve your messaging and use specific mediums to attract your ideal prospect. I'm going to tell you again; this is the part that excites me. I love to share this because this is business, baby! We're not writing *Harry Potter* it's not a dry textbook, and thank God it's not a computer manual. **It is your Nonfiction Lead & Profit Generating Business Book—*in eight weeks!***

What is the story you're telling? It is the greatest sales tool you can leverage even further! And a book isn't just ANOTHER medium to do that. It is one of the oldest mediums that continually takes advantage and leverages this fact.

When you're an author, you're positioned as an authority, and done right; you will be positioned as THE authority in your niche.

Caveat, *This is beyond powerful, and it is where I further differentiate myself and draw a line. As I mentioned earlier about needing to have the right heart, I don't work with anyone that doesn't already deserve to be there and isn't already at a certain level. In most cases, they simply need some guidance and accountability.*

Look, with enough Photoshop, lights, cameras, and professional photography, anyone in the world can LOOK like a rockstar, but not everyone can BE the rockstar, like yourself. To be clear, I'm not saying take some mud, throw it against the wall, throw a cover on it and upload it to Amazon.

It's much more profound and personal for me. I take this process very seriously. I know every one of our authors feels it and knows you can't just buy it or fake your most significant transformations, milestones, and turning points.

Your business book will position your authority, credibility, and trust factor much higher than it currently is. While you're already at a certain level, there are new audiences that aren't yet on your radar, and you're not on theirs simply because you're not in the publishing world or as far into it as you could and should be—*yet.*

I, however, would be happy to tell you how they can find you. I can show you where to find them and introduce you to them.

This is not an and-or thing. This is a synergistic approach to taking what's already working for you, enhancing it, and creating a *"YES"* thing. Change from choosing this OR that to deciding if you want to do something or not because you have an asset in place that can work for you. Instead of you having to repeat yourself over and over or being the linchpin, everything revolves around.

The advantages are many. That two-day shelf life of a business card is now a two-plus-year shelf-life with your book.

That one sheet now says *"author and speaker."*

The person on the plane you wanted to talk to now can get to know you even better than arguably some of those *"closest"* to you, might currently know you by the time you land.

The fundraiser looking for incentives for the donors now has a tangible item, instead of another one of one-hundred *"FREE Consultations" given to the recipient on printer paper, made ten minutes before the bidding.* Your dream prospect you haven't been able to reach is now only some simple postage away. Your dream guest for your show may reach out to YOU.

I could list dozens and dozens, if not hundreds, of scenarios and opportunities, but I keep hearing *Aladdin's: "A Whole New World."*

It's just that, a whole new world, you're either not in, or not as frequent as you could, and should be, that's profitable, a lot of fun, and the caliber of people is higher.

If that's what, and who you're attracted to, I hope you're as excited to start the plan as much as I'm excited to continue to share it.

Some of these also apply to publicity, but what kind of great *#FirstWorldProblem* is it when there are so many benefits that you have a 3x, 4x, or 5x opportunity for leverage?

Grab a pen if you haven't already because you're going to get more done now than you likely have–*in this department*–in the last year.

*"If you fail to plan,
you are planning to fail!"*

~ *Benjamin Franklin*

Plan

DAYS 1-3 *(7 MAX)* WEEK 1

You will be starting the first half of the plan right from the start, and the *"writing"* as soon as possible—*at the latest starting day one of week two.*

LAYING A STRONG FOUNDATION WITH THE PLANNING AND PROMOTION FOR THE PUBLISHING OF YOUR BUSINESS BOOK (Part I)

I hope you're enjoying the ride so far—*because the roller coaster has some fun dips, curves, loops, and inversions coming right up!* This is one part of the book I've had to come back to multiple times, so it's as straightforward as possible for you in written form—*since some jumps do occur with my method.*

Again this is intentional, as it leverages time compounding, so you can profit and make an impact sooner, rather than later. You will, however, have to keep paying attention and follow the steps in order, especially as they start to stack.

Rest assured, it's temporary. There are only two sides to the coin—*Planning and Promotion.* All of which I will gift wrap with a beautiful bow by the end, and I'll leave you with only one. **Promotion.**

Here's the workflow:

1. Idea
2. Process
3. Title
4. Subtitle
5. *"Writing it"*
6. Announcing it
7. *"Writing it"* some more
8. Editing
9. Formatting
10. Publish *(Chapter 4)*
11. Publicity *(Chapter 5)*
12. Profit *(Chapter 6)*

IDEA

Let's start here.

Most books never get off the ground because of statements such as, *"I have so many things I could write about."* Welcome to the club, you've done something with your life, congratulations. Pick one.

Focusing is a significant reason we don't need 401 weeks to write this book. **What's your business?**

Great, that's your topic, and your idea will be centered around it.

Our goal is to add value and serve your prospects while generating new leads and profits. *We're still in agreement on that, right?* Good. Don't over-complicate this. I helped my good friend and now fellow publisher colleague, Jenn, come up with her table of contents, walking from one end of the hotel to the other after speaking at an event. I'm sure we stayed a few minutes once we got there, and of course, she tweaked it before the final print, but when I say keep it simple, I mean it.

I'm the CEO of IWDNow Marketing & Publishing.

- How do I help you?
- Business Book Marketing & Publishing.
- What's the focus of my book?
- Business Book Marketing & Publishing.

My ideal prospect is: **YOU!**

If you want to plan to WIN, grab that pen again, and fill this in:

My business is: _____

I help people by: _____

My core business focus is: _____

My ideal prospect is: _____

Great news! You've started your book! Now announce it!

Brainstorm in more detail what your core business really is:

_____

Brainstorm in more detail who your ideal prospect really is:

_____

Look at the first four boxes above—*not the expanded detail.* At their core, these will be the starting point for your title and subtitle.

With not just an honorable mention but a standing ovation, I am excited to introduce you to!

PROCESS

We're now talking about your unique value proposition, more than likely your IP—*the differentiator,* and the core reason you have your business—*which others might try to imitate.*

_____

_____

_____

_____

_____

My process is:

Brainstorm 10 plus steps for the outline of your process, for your business book:

_____

_____

_____

_____

_____

_____

_____

_____

_____

_____

_____

_____

_____

_____

_____

_____

_____

If you have more than ten steps, feel free to add them, but you really don't need more. *List everything you think you need now, and we can refine it later.*

For example, with publishing, there could be 137 plus steps in the process. For the sake of the book, does me saying, *"Seventeen days after you announce your book, make another announcement"* mean there are two steps or just a continuation of one? What if I say, *"Announcing it on text, video, and with an image!"* Is it now three steps every day, times 30 days? Is it for 90 steps, or is it one, *"Publicity?"*

List them all now, but we will keep it simple, *nobody wants to read 148 chapters.*

It is my sincerest prayer you see this isn't rocket science, and the answers are already inside of you. It's my duty to get your expertise from your head onto the paper.

TITLE

Here is where the fun comes in, your title might be the company name, it might be the company method, it might be the company process, such as Kirk's #1 Best Seller:

> *"Rescue Site AED Program™: The 5 Critical Components of a Life-Saving AED Program"*
>
> **~ Kirk Mote**

It might be the benefits promise to your prospects like:

> *"An Immigrant in the C-Suite: From the Journey, Lessons for the Business Community"*
>
> **~ Dr. John Lopez**

Similarly, as we did with:

> *"Unstoppable: 7 Steps to Becoming a More Intentional Leader"*
>
> **~ Rocio Perez**

Rocio Perez serves the Latin-America community, and a month after launching her first book, we had it translated for the Spanish market:

"IMPARABLE: 7 Pasos Para Convertirse En Un Líder Más Proactivo" (Spanish Edition)

~ Rocio Perez

One of my late authors—*may she rest in peace,* who I'm still so very proud of:

"Wealth Building for the Aspiring Entrepreneur: How to Start Building Your Legacy Now!"

~ Manola Webster

The late Manola was a great woman with an intense passion for helping others build their legacy of wealth. It is unfortunate that she passed shortly after publishing—*and way too soon.* I will never forget when I asked, *"How does it feel?"* and she said, **"This is the first book, that's all mine."**

You can have a book with other people—*an anthology,* collaboration is great. Maybe it makes sense at some point for you. **Nothing, however, can top a book that is all yours.** It leaves you with such an incredible feeling of accomplishment and pride—*I promise you that.*

I just checked Manola's Facebook—
www.ExpertAuthorityEffect.com/ManolaTribute, and as I write this sentence, I can still see all she was doing and everything we were ramping up to do.

While I'm sad she's gone, I'm so honored she trusted me and chose me to bring her vision to life. While she may not physically be here, her legacy still lives on through her book, friends, and family that she left behind. You're very much still missed Manola, THANK YOU for your trust and the opportunity to serve you.

Take any of my business books:

"Video Marketing for Business Owners: The Ultimate 7 Step Guide to Become the Expert, Authority and Celebrity in Your Niche"

~ Mario Fachini

Take one guess as to what it's about, who it is for, how many steps the process has, and the promise that will be delivered.

"The IWDNow Freedom Platform™: The World's #1 System to Build WordPress Websites Automatically!"

~ Mario Fachini

...again, I don't need to expand on it. It works.

"The Expert Authority Effect™: Your 7-Step Brain Dead Simple Blueprint to Attract Your Ideal Dream Clients by Increasing Your Authority Positioning Today!"

~ Mario Fachini

...is there any confusion?

I want you to know it's not that hard to title your book. You already have the answer. This formula has worked for me since 2012, I share it with all of our concierge-level author clients, and now I'm excited to share it with you. I used it in my last book from 2016:

"The Expert Authority Effect™: Your 7-Step Brain Dead Simple Blueprint to Attract Your Ideal Dream Clients by Increasing Your Authority Positioning Today!"

~ Mario Fachini

It worked then too, and it still works today.

I will never forget when Bill Benner came to me and wanted help publishing and launching his book:

"LASER SCANNERS: TECHNOLOGIES AND APPLICATIONS: How they work, and how they can work for your product"

~ William Benner

He had it written, as you may also, but you know there's more involved. Your manuscript is a GREAT start, but it's not published. Without proper promotion, you'll never *"Launch"* it. Don't get stuck here. It's almost worse than not starting the book.

The real honor was when Bill called back and said his son was ready, wanted to have an advantage in the sports realm, and I was the first publisher he thought of that he trusted. He loved my method even more than, let's say, *"some others."* I didn't take this lightly, as I never have, and I'm not going to with you either.

I'm proud to now present to you:

"THE WORLD OF YOUTH BASKETBALL: A parent's guide through your child's journey"

~ Will Benner

I remember when we took Will through my method, suggesting *"parents"* and *"your"* to hit closer to home, instead of something to the effect of *"A guide through the child's journey."* The book isn't for the child. The book is for the parents, and it's not just any child. It is YOUR child.

I hope your wheels are starting to spin, or you have at least turned the car on.

Whether you use the company name or not, already have a process— *or would like to see how easy it is creating one.* You can always lead with the promise of the benefits you're going to deliver, like Leora, Don, and Adel:

"Ace Your C-Suite Interview: International Headhunter Reveals Insider Strategies for Executive Job Search, Tips to Master Interviewing, Negotiating Better Salaries, and Getting Hired Fast!"

~ Leora Bach

"The Ultimate Consumer Awareness Guide: Everything You Need to Know About How to Properly Select the Right Carpet or Flooring - But Didn't Know To Ask!"

~ Don Lovato

"Celebrity Media Secrets: 7 Simple Steps to Present with Power, Poise, and Style On-Camera, Get Booked on TV and Media and Become a Celebrity in Your Industry"

~ Adel Wilson

These are just some of the books we helped publish. I'm going to move to the next point because every time I think of one, I remember the story, author, process, and what it did for them within a few short weeks, too a few short months directly after publishing—*on top of 10 others that *while not guaranteed...had similar results...since they listened and followed my* **Expert Authority Effect™ Publishing Method.**

Your title will be a fluid concept for the next eight weeks—*while we continue to go through the process, don't feel it has to be perfect day one, but realize there are real deadlines, and it's best if you have done the final title refinement before you go to print.*

Remember, it doesn't need to be done all at once. ***How good does it feel to understand not only what it takes but realize it's a lot less complicated than you thought?***

Brainstorm 10 plus ideas for the title of your business book:

Don't be afraid to screw up, make mistakes, or not have it perfected on the first go around. It's about getting your ideas out, and the process started.

Below are literally the notes, just copied and pasted from what started as ideas to now being a legitimate book that is already over 18,000 plus words and 50% complete. I'm already up to Chapter 4 just below this—*simply because I kept expanding on this one sentence:*

The Expert Authority Effect™ Publishing Method

And that's all you need as well—*the end result,* the promise you can and will deliver, your expertise on paper, and I will continue to guide you through it.

Mario's Manuscript Mirror Mode

~~Perspective,~~ ~~Prepare~~, Plan, ~~Perform,~~ ~~Press,~~ Publicity/

I was brainstorming potential keywords that make the most sense for my method.

You can see I used two in order to refine the steps in my method further—*and the other four were voted off the island.*

The Expert Authority Effect™ Publishing Method:

The name was nearly instant, and yours may be as well—*or at least start you at 80% in the process.* While not required, I would encourage you to look at your process. You may already have the IP and not even be aware. If you want to have a quick chat on expert authority positioning, we're more than happy to, but first, I invite you to look at what was never even a consideration:

"How to write a book for your business."
"Self-Publish on Amazon with ease."
"Publishing Power for Profit"
"Get Your Book on Amazon Today"
"If you don't have a book on Amazon, you're not in business."

Do you see how vague all of these are? Throwing in some buzz words doesn't make it any more unique. There is only one on the list that isn't completely unfortunate looking. While still not good, and definitely not great, it is not entirely awful.

Here are my thoughts on why these are weak—*and you shouldn't even consider them:*

"How to write a book for your business."

Well, why would I even care or want to?

"Self-Publish on Amazon with Ease."

So, you said *"Self-Publish"* instead of a book? Bravo, but you never told me why I should care, so who cares if it's hard or *"with ease?"*

"Publishing Power for Profit"

This is the one that's not entirely awful. While making good use of alliteration, it fails to tell me the benefit for my business. Marketing Power for Profit, Entrepreneur Power for Profit, Car Power for Profit— *could mean running people off the road, as an airport "efficiency" campaign for rideshare companies.* We don't have any further details as to how or why, again it doesn't SOUND horrible, but it still fails because we can't prove the benefits. I talk about this in my **Expert Authority Effect™ Messaging Audio Training Program**, and just like in a court case, *it's not what you can say but what you can prove.*

"Get Your Book on Amazon Today"

This could also be called *"take any Word doc over 24 pages and upload it to Amazon"* because that's how you could deliver on that promise. I highly, highly, highly, don't recommend it, but if you just don't care, I have a dummy manuscript you're welcome to have because, I kid you not, that's literally all it takes. I recommend, like Dad used to tell me, *"doing it right the first time, so that way you don't have to go back again."* Again, too vague, there are no real benefits, and I'm still left asking questions. It's a nice attempt at amateur copywriting. *"Today."* Ohhhh snap, I better rush to get it. It appears that someone read a blog post on *"words that create urgency."*—*I'm rolling my eyes if you haven't pictured that or smirked a little already.*

"If you don't have a book on Amazon, you're not in business."

This is another typical amateur marketing maneuver. It's the *"If you don't comply with the one trick I know, you're wrong."* I also find it highly insulting. The reality is most of the books on Amazon DON'T have a business by which they are backed. It is the same regurgitated information parroted everywhere else. They are not earning six, seven, or eight-plus figures, BUT they did figure out how to upload the document on Amazon and slap together a cover, so one could give credit where credit is due, but it would be a failing credit. Shockingly, that makes them in the top 10% somehow.

I honestly believe every business should have a book—*including yours.* I know what it's done for my clients and me. You may not know all the required steps, and that's completely okay—*you have the only one you really need, desire to share your expertise.* You were successful before you read this, and you'll continue to be successful after because it's you, your expertise, experience, and how you think, NOT because you uploaded a single blog or LinkedIn post to Amazon and hit print. I do know, however, when done correctly, your business book will further capitalize on everything you already are and will continue to be.

As I've mentioned, don't get overly creative here. **Use your existing marketing and processes to get started and finish.**

We will refine and continue to refine from there. It has far more to do with adding value to your prospects than hitting one magic word, whether it's in the book or on the cover.

Note: As not to directly insult anyone while merely making an example, I did not look on Amazon for any of those titles, or the Internet, or Google. If one happens to be yours, it wasn't intentional, and well, I'm glad you're reading my book now since clearly, it needed some work.

It was, however, extremely easy to come up with them, as I've helped thousands of companies with marketing over the last decade, and most marketing fails basic, simple tests, naming is one of them, and I've even done similar exercises with my in-person audiences.

I ask everyone to pass forward their business cards, flyers, and promotional content they have on them. During webinars and livestreams, it's even easier to scour the interwebs to find how they REALLY APPEAR to their prospects.

100% of the time, we are simply *"too close,"* myself included. That is why I've had dozens of people on my own team comb through every last thing we can think of, all of whom have different *"lenses"* they see the world through, and while from different backgrounds, they are all specialized experts in their respective fields, and I trust them.

That's why I'm here with you, staying in my lane, and **Expert Authority Effect™ Genius Zone**, helping you.

Remember, the title should be short, sweet, and to the point. Now let's elaborate on the promise of the sub-title.

SUB-TITLE:

"The Easiest, Fastest & Most Profitable Way to Publish Your Non-Fiction Business Book"

Not bad. The car is moving.

"The Easiest, Fastest & Most Profitable Way to Publish Your Non-Fiction Business Book in 8 Weeks or Less"

Fastest was too generic. You want to be specific. It did remind me that I never say *"fastest."* If you asked me out loud in person, I would say, *"Publish your business book in less than 8-weeks."* Also, it's now getting a little long.

"The Easiest, Fastest & Most Profitable Way to Publish Your Non-Fiction Lead Generating Business Book"

I added *"Lead Generating"* after realizing I also said this in real life.

"The Easiest Way to Publish Your Non-Fiction Lead & Profit Generating Business Book"

I dropped *"Fastest"* and added *"Non-Fiction"* and *"Profit"* since I also have said this in real life. Are you noticing a pattern?

"The Simplest Way to Publish Your Non-Fiction Lead & Profit Generating Business Book in 8 Weeks or Less"

I changed *"Easiest"* to *"Simplest"* since the process isn't easy. That's why most people don't do it, they're average, and we're not. I also added *"8 Weeks"* back because it replaces *"Fastest."* I always say it in person and from the stage because it's one of the critical differentiators, from my business to many others.

"The Simplest Way to Publish Your Non-Fiction Lead & Profit Generating Professional Business Book in 8-Weeks or Less"

I liked it but didn't love it. I don't like things I don't love, especially if they're going to be around forever. What I was going for was another modifier to differentiate that it's not only a book, but a business book, and not merely a business book, but a professional business book. In retrospect, *"High-Quality"* would have been more the word I was going for, but again, we're brainstorming, don't judge. **Write, get it out, and the right one will find it's way home.**

Caveat—I just typed the below section and came back to this, and I'm smirking since I already said, "The title is done." This is the fun of going through my method. It's not done until it's done, so this "high quality" either made it's way to the title, or it didn't. You already know the outcome before I do. How surreal is that?

Certain words or phrases may make the title too long and have too many words. This is where you rely on other elements to tell you the same thing without using that word. In my case, the examples are: The font, colors, pen, design, everything about it, really should scream *"business book publishing"*—so I don't have to. The same is true for yours.

I will tell you what I tell all our authors: *"Put it to a vote."* Marketing is quickly testing and implementing valuable data. You can always veto and have the final say, but don't be shy about asking. A side benefit of asking for a vote is that it gets your prospects engaged in the process. It is excellent marketing to not just focus on the details of the launch itself but also get your readers engaged, join you throughout the process, and experience the fun.

Now, I doubt it's made it to the final, but you have already read and know the correct answer, and I don't. Kinda cool.

While even on your first title naming try, you have a 50/50 shot— *and yes, I did phone a friend, as well as ask the audience.* You even have a bonus option I didn't, *"Ask the Author."*

"The Simplest Way to Publish Your Nonfiction Lead & Profit Generating Business Book in Less than 8-Weeks"

Short of adding *"and print it,"* I don't think I could have made the title much longer, and that's why it's on the cutting room floor.

"7-Steps to Publish Your Non-Fiction Lead & Profit Generating Business Book in Less than 8-Weeks"

The *"Simplest"* is still in the title. It's just not said, as I have taught for over a decade, making the vague specific. *"7 Steps"* was added. As it always is, I didn't start with it because maybe it would be 5, 10, or

12 steps—*it's brainstorming.* Also, *"Less than"* was removed because it's just taking up two more words. If *"8 Weeks"* doesn't impress you, *"Less than"* isn't a game-changer. It might even cause you anxiety—*which is the opposite of what I want for you.*

Now is the moment you've been waiting for:

Drum-roll Please

Grand Finale Sub-Title:

"7 Steps to Publish Your Nonfiction Lead & Profit-Generating Business Book in 8 Weeks."

It turns out *"7-Steps,"* and *"8-Weeks,"* are wrong, as well as *"Profit Generating"*—*cool, thank you for the help public vote.* With that, my friend, the title is done!

The entire sub-title process took:

- Six days based on the timestamps of the mock-up cover graphics variations
- Eight days based on the LIVE social media announcements.

Detailed Timeline:

Day 1, Week 1 | Announced it to the world.

Day 2, Week 1 | Replied with *"Thank You's"* to *"Congrats!"* messages.

Day 3, Week 1 | Version 1 & 2 - Started cover artwork variations, asked for feedback with an emphasis on subtitle naming.

Day 4, Week 1 | Version 3 & 4 - Refined.

Day 2, Week 2 | Version 5 & 6 - Subtitle required no additional tweaks; essentially, it was complete.

Day 3, Week 3 - *Onward!* | The subtitle was still complete. Focus, however, shifted to continue the graphic design variations.

As you can see, it doesn't really matter where you start. It's where you finish. We're going to do the one thing most people don't take the time to do: **START!**

Brainstorm 10 plus ideas for the sub-title of your business book:

_____

_____

_____

_____

_____

_____

_____

_____

_____

_____

_____

_____

_____

_____

_____

_____

_____

_____

I remember walking Manola through her process. I'll never forget the 15-20 minutes we cranked out her title, sub-title, and table of contents outline before we ended the call—*and I have the video to prove it.* I have a gift for you at the end, so if you want to see it, don't think I'm going to leave you hanging.

The reality is the title and sub-title won't *"make"* great content into a book. However, if you don't invest some thought, insight, and commitment to refine, it could break it.

You must understand what works, and don't try to reinvent the wheel. The answer will come to you, and one of those days—*you'll just know and be done with it.*

Then I will say, *"Very good, what did you do today to promote it?"*

A book is no different than any other area of business, and it comes down to what I go into further detail in one of my other books, **The Expert Authority Effect™**:

- Market
- Message
- Medium
- Model

You have to ask yourself:

- Who's my ideal reader?
- What's the message I'm sending them?
- On what medium?
- What's my business model for sustainability?

If any of those break down in your business or book, you're building your foundation on a house of cards—*while an interesting show, I don't want you to be the "best-kept secret."* I **want you to achieve your goal, get the results, and add value to your audience. Period. Bar none. Case closed.**

I have countless examples of people who talk a lot and have nothing to say. When I published my first book in 2012, these were people who said, *"I've always WANTED to write a book."* Well, I did it, and they **STILL** want to.

The Expert Authority Effect™ Publishing Method is all about getting your business book finished in the fastest, most efficient, and profitable fashion. Every year I re-evaluate what we will implement to *"run faster"* and *"trim the fat,"* and every year, I smile and think to myself, *"This is pretty good."* Sure I tweak it here and there, enhancing the marketing strategy, but often I intentionally remove more and more at the core. I strip it down, so it's digestible at every step of the process. I want you to accomplish everything in a matter of hours each week. I've designed my method with your prospects and business in mind. I don't want you taking any unnecessary time to fumble around. I would rather have you invest your time deliberately where it will pay you dividends and do so in a fast, efficient, profitable manner so you can continue to enjoy your time freedom.

When you do the steps from **The Expert Authority Effect™ Publishing Method** in the proper order and at the right time, you will be creating a compounding synergistic effect—*How else do you think we're pulling this off in eight weeks? It's not by spending nine months thinking about it, six months brainstorming it, three months outlining it, two months refining it, and the day of publishing it, talking about it, heaven forbid launching it.*

"WRITING IT"

You have the title, the subtitle, and there is yet to be a business without a process. You have outlined your chapters, you walk people through it, and you do what I'm doing now. You document as you go. If you've never done it before, starting today, slow down, breathe, and realize everything you do from here until bedtime tonight is data. It is content that you are CREATING at a supercomputer level.

Harness the innate power you already have.

You have another unfair advantage. Like me, you're the expert at your craft. You've done it hundreds and thousands of times, and you may not even realize it.

Have no fear!

We're going to extract it all right now with the: **Expert Authority Effect™ Evidence Intelligence Gathering Process.**

The three stages of Intelligence Gathering—*none of which are limited to the bullet points listed here. Let's get creative!*

- **Low Hanging Fruit**

These are incredibly prevalent assets that are so common you are probably oblivious to them. You will see them now since I'm talking about them.

- **Everyday Exceptional**

These are relatively common assets, maybe not at arm's reach, but on the shelf, nearby, or in that folder.

- **Worth Their Weight in Gold**

These assets are worth their weight in gold. Unfortunately, you've buried them—*maybe not six feet under, but we're going to have to dust off that shovel to dig them up.*

If you don't have LastPass **(www.ExpertAuthorityEffect.com/LastPass)** *open right now, you should. Ask your assistant and start thinking about logins to accounts because this is where these assets are hiding.*

Let's start with the low hanging fruit by grabbing the nearest:

- **Business Card**
- **Flyer**
- **Pen | Calendar | Ruler | Document**
- **A-Team**
- **Interviews**
- **Awards**
- **And much more.**

Even if these were gone, all you were left with was your expertise, and today was day number one. I have no doubt that in thirty days, you could re-create a large chunk of it because the power isn't in the award or the testimonial. ***The power is in YOU!***

We simply need to keep bringing it out of you, polish it off, and have you shine brighter than ever.

Any area that you shine in is fair game for book ideas and content.

That cute infographic you had your designer make for the sole purpose of a social media post, while arguably may be applied to the wrong *"MEDIUM,"* by no means has any less value. It very well might just hold your table of contents—*or an 80-90% version of it.* Gather all of this. ***There are no rules about what it is or where it came from if it's 100% legitimately yours. It's still yours, and it's fair game.***

This is how I wrote my second book in a day, third in under five days, starting Wednesday night and continuing over the Thanksgiving holiday weekend. I did this while I was still present with family and friends. I was ready to give it to the printer Monday morning. Additionally, I didn't work on Thanksgiving, and it wasn't "work." I jotted down some thoughts here and there, re-organized it, celebrated, and called it a day.

The book I'm referring to is **The Expert Authority Effect™**. I sold a lot of copies. People still buy it. People still love it. It's a killer-looking hardcover that pushed the envelope. I invite you to read it—*after you write your book, of course.* It will help give you clarity on your marketing message and systems to grow your business.

It's only been a few hours, and Microsoft Word shows that I have just under 6,000 words. I know I mentioned a larger number earlier in the book, *"how's that,"* you wonder? As I mentioned prior, jumping around when *"writing"* content isn't only allowed, it's encouraged. I prefer Evernote and Basecamp, in conjunction with video and audio for *"writing,"* but that's me. There are dozens of ways that I will be sharing the best of the best as you continue reading. You do you. Just get it done.

I copied and pasted to check the word count for you. I am on track to beat my last goal of five days with three to four, but if I take two days off, does that still count as five days? Just keep going, and dive into your **Expert Authority Effect™ Genius Zone,** and the floodgates will open, and the years and decades of expertise will just make it out of your head onto your manuscript. Let it out. It's meant to be free. Prior to this, it was most likely under leveraged at best anyhow. This is another synergistic leverage point I've taught for years that starts with what I call:

BLOCK15TIME™

When you break your time into 15-minute blocks, you now have 96 opportunities a day to make an epic life happen. In my experience, it only takes one or two for four to six to occur very naturally and without you noticing.

When you're in your **Expert Authority Effect™ Genius Zone**, you don't want any distracting time to occur. When you're writing a book, you don't want three, four, or five-minute intervals. You want all your thoughts to flow together without having to re-read for 20 minutes worth of what you just wrote, to figure out where you left off, only to have to dive in STILL, to get back in the groove.

Here's the deal, once it's done, it's done. I find solace knowing regardless of whatever time it is right now and how much has passed, once this is done, it will be at least a year, maybe more, before I do this again. You don't need to every two months or six, for that matter. You are not in the business of having to write dozens and dozens of books.

You're already doing a book, if it makes sense, sure, by all means, I have, but I advise you to go deeper with what you already made a priority once.

Decide from the start that you want it to be a *"best written,"* as well as a *"bestseller,"* and truthfully, bestseller doesn't even have to be a goal. Most go for the gold star. It's nice, thankful, but the impact on the people and businesses I've helped transform that's more exciting. The good news is you can have both.

Don't let someone produce junk that reflects poorly on you, your brand, and your company. Make no mistake, you sitting on your high-horse with no line of people waiting to pay you for a ride is even worse for business.

I'm going to reiterate my earlier phrase, *"Don't over-complicate this."* It is already inside of you, every last word, and there is a VERY HIGH LIKELIHOOD. A lot of it is already out of you.

Save yourself three months, and leverage Block15Time™. Let's play a game!—*Great time to invite your team to join if you haven't done so already,* to see HOW MUCH you can come up with!

Let's continue to the next stage of the *Expert Authority Effect*™ **Evidence Intelligence Gathering**™ **Process:**

EVERYDAY EXCEPTIONAL

You will be full of ideas of where to find what. Other high leverage areas to go to first are:

- **Success stories**
- **People with a positive interaction**
- **FAQ's** *(frequently asked questions)*
- **EAQ's** *(expert authority questions)*
- **LinkedIn articles**
- **LinkedIn posts**
- **Facebook long-form posts**
- **Facebook posts**

The goal is to create a melting pot of ideas to have a framework composed of the best ideas that you can choose to use or lose. This way, you will not need to write for an entire quarter, two, or heaven forbid three—*or more*. You only need to come up with what you've already done in incremental efforts for other promotional items throughout your business.

Let's move on to the last stage of the **Expert Authority Effect**™ **Evidence Intelligence Gathering Process:**

Worth Their Weight in Gold

- **Internal guides**
- **Internal checklists**
- **Public checklists**
- **Public guides**
- **Your best clients**
- **Existing clients**
- **Potential prospects**
- **Collaborations**

- **Interviews**
- **Podcasts**
- **Speaking from stage**
- **Sponsorships**
- **Video testimonials**
- **Audio testimonials**
- **Written testimonials**

and last but not least, one of my absolute favorites and 99% of the time overlooked—*or at least never leveraged:*

- **SOCIAL MEDIA COMMENTS!**

Do you remember about four seconds ago when I mentioned *"Social Media Posts"* in Everyday Exceptional? When was the last time you intentionally and strategically collected screenshots of the great things people said about your company?

Sure, you get them, notice them, and you should be replying, but do you LEVERAGE them?

You don't need to wait until your next live event or for them to walk into your business, to get a video testimonial from them. Every day you have positive, third-party, unsolicited, genuine content being created on every single social platform on earth. This content is conveyed publicly, as well as your messages privately. I consider any sincere praise or industry recognition you receive fair game, and I advise you to leverage it to your benefit and honor those who are genuine.

DO NOT treat this as just another comment or message. It's not. It's what we refer to in the marketing world as *"Social Proof."*

When you feel like you've gathered it all, then you're done. Your brain will go to work FOR YOU. You can also engage your team. Put everyone on alert to go on the treasure hunt with you. The more hands-on-deck, the better. Candidly, what I'm referring to here is the feeling of *"diminishing returns."* There will be a point where it will be best for one, or just a few, of your team members to dive deep into *"covert six mode"* and find every last thing they can to add to your arsenal.

You will achieve the 80% point—*80/20 Rule* rather quickly within 7-10 days. YOU don't have to go Nicholas Cage's National Treasure, but part of your team should. I'm also confident in asking:

"Is this the first time ever you've done this?"
"Have you attempted it in the last calendar year?"

Would you like me to guess your answer?

Hopefully, you've never been audited financially. Still, my guess is you've never done an internal marketing message audit, and if so, it wasn't as thorough as it could have been, and even if it was *"decent,"* it's been a minute—*or decade-plus.*

The best thing you can do from this sentence onward is to make it a weekly, at the very least monthly priority that your NEW Social Proof is continuously collected moving forward. You can simply maintain it with minimal effort instead of spiking once a year and then forgetting about it. Create the habit now. This one new habit alone, I have no doubt, could be worth millions to your business. Going back to the premise of *"keeping it simple,"* how much have you already done that outside of the book is just collecting dust? You don't need to answer. I can see the look on your face. Just commit to stopping the problem today.

Here are more exact notes I grabbed from writing this book, as you saw with the subtitle earlier when I took myself through the **Expert Authority Effect™ Evidence Intelligence Gathering™ Process:**[1] [2]

---

1   **Mario's Manuscript Mirror Mode**

"Authority" The root of the word is "Author."

1. Idea

2. Title

3. Subtitle

4. Cover mock-up

5. Announce it

6. Pre-sale link Pricing | (Paperback/Hardcover) / Royalties

2   **ABOUT**

Simply jot some stuff down and keep building on it. Your editors will make sure it all makes sense later.

There is no limit to from where you can derive inspiration. We live in an abundant world. Inspiration is everywhere.

If you only get one bullet point from this, it should be:

"Use everything you possibly can, that you already have done, to your advantage."

Speaking of advantages, the process points you write below will also become the start of your table of contents (TOC).

Brainstorm 10 plus main process points from the Expert Authority Effect™ Evidence Intelligence Gathering™ Process for your business book

---

Whatever doesn't make it to the TOC will be leveraged for content INSIDE your book.

Now copy the main Process Points from above and write them below while you start to:

Brainstorm three bullet points in addition to each of your main process points for your business book

1. **Main Process Point 1**

   * _____
   * _____
   * _____

2. **Main Process Point 2**

   * _____
   * _____
   * _____

3. **Main Process Point 3**

   * _____
   * _____
   * _____

4. **Main Process Point 4**

   * _____
   * _____
   * _____

5. **Main Process Point 5**

    - _____

    - _____

    - _____

6. **Main Process Point 6**

    - _____

    - _____

    - _____

7. **Main Process Point 7**

    - _____

    - _____

    - _____

8. **Main Process Point 8**

    - _____

    - _____

    - _____

9. **Main Process Point 9**

    - _____

    - _____

    - _____

10. Main Process Point 10

- _____
- _____
- _____

Oh, you're an overachiever, are you? Better get the butter, baby, because you're on a roll! Keep going, don't feel you NEED to use all three, or limit yourself to only three. The priority is that you keep getting your expertise on paper!

11. Additional Potential Process Point

- _____
- _____
- _____

12. Additional Potential Process Point

- _____
- _____

13. Additional Potential Process Point

- _____
- _____
- _____

14. Additional Potential Process Point

- _____
- _____
- _____

15. Additional Potential Process Point

- _____
- _____
- _____

While I'd never encourage your reticence, I'd be remiss not finishing this book and only selling you what may be simply perceived as a ream of paper.

Do you see now, however, when appropriately done, how quickly you can rapidly prototype this whole thing out?

I mentioned previously that some of my books took one to five days. This one is already on track with 18,000 plus words, with a goal of 35,000-40,000 words, 45,000 total words max. So far, it's only been four days, and I took a complete day off yesterday. While I'm confident I could say _"five days"_ again, it will be at least six because of taking one day off. I've already decided that even with aiming to be done two days earlier, I can polish this pearl more than I ever have and still take two days off while still completing it within a week.

If we broke this down to hours, I have just under four total 24-hour period time blocks, using Block15Time™.

With every fiber of my being, I can confidently tell you that if you want to:

"You can do this in a week or less."

I will also tell you that...

"You should do it."

I have designed this portion to allow for two to three weeks for _"writing."_ You can take four weeks maximum, even though you don't need it.

"ANNOUNCING IT" *(and SELLING IT)*

Day 1, Week 1

You gain the maximum amount of time, most fun, and profit.

Day 1, Week 2

A significant lead, still fun and profitable.

Day 1, Week 3 *(AT THE LATEST)*

No less than thirty days from launch, *spread your wings and fly!* You don't need any more info. You need heart—*as we covered in Chapter 1: PURPOSE.* There is nothing to fear. You have the **Expert Authority Effect™ Publishing Method** to catch you. It's going to be more than okay; it's going to be the time of your life. I need you to trust me and jump. Announcing your book in many ways is the real beginning.

I look forward to seeing you on your launch day, and it starts with announcing it. *I invite you to use @MarioFachini and our #EAEPublishingMethod hashtag so we can join in the celebration.*

Hello, time compounding! You beautiful creature, thanks for helping make my book possible.

Now that we have shed months off of the process, from here on out, as you keep writing, you also must keep selling. When companies hire me for consulting, I always ask, *"How many offers do you make a day, a week, a month?"* I often hear, *"What do you mean?"*

Therein lies the problem.

While I've never promised or guaranteed I will "make you a bestselling author," I can say with a very high degree of certainty when you follow **The Expert Authority Effect™ Publishing Method,** *there is an above-average probability that within 24-48 hours of launching, there is an excellent chance you will be able to add more to your title's positioning in addition to "published" author.*

I DO KNOW, and CAN SAY with 1000% certainty, you will NEVER be a "Best Selling" anything ...if you don't sell, or "sell it" for "FREE."

Books are no exception. Most of our authors finish in two to three weeks. I budget for a maximum of around four weeks with my method. Do your best and get it done. There is still:

- *"Writing It"* some more
- Editing
- Formatting
- Publishing
- Printing
- Fulfilling
- Promoting
- Profiting
- *Did I mention the in-person live event VIP Book Signing!?*

Essentially, the first thirty days are for writing. The second set of thirty days is for: *editing, promoting, formatting, publishing, and promotion leading up to launch day.* At that point, the workload drastically drops down from expertise extraction, as we shift gears into evergreen promotion and enhanced book sales strategies.

While we can start pretty much anything at any time, for the sake of a 30,000-foot view:

- **30 days = Writing**
- **30 days = Promotion**
- **1 day = Launch**

Now you may be thinking: *"Wait a second, eight weeks = 54 days; how does that equal 61?"*

It doesn't.

There is overlap—*a lot.*

In all fairness, I also gave you a heads up at the beginning of this chapter to keep your lap bar tightly fastened. There are still more turns ahead. The reality is, I've done launches:

- **With books entirely written, and more than seven weeks of promotion**
- **The book is still being written during weeks six and seven**
- **The day before the author is traveling**

You might think I'm crazy, but for all I know, you're lazy. There is a reason most people never even complete their first book, let alone multiple books, nor do they make a real impact on the world. They miss the opportunity to amaze themselves.

Like I did with one of Don's other books that I haven't even mentioned, three weeks was the fastest any of my clients have written their book from start to finish, **following The Expert Authority Effect™ Publishing Method**, for one of his other businesses at the time: December 8th-30th, 2014. Congrats again, Don.

Here is the paraphrase of our conversation at the end of his marketing consulting call with me:

Don: *"I want to launch my fitness book before the new year."*
Me: *"You know that's less than a month away, right?"*
Don: *"Yeah"*
Me: *"Let's do it."*

...so we did.

- **If you already have a book written, good, you need to promote it.**
- **If you have it somewhat written, good, you need to promote it**
- **If you don't have anything written, good, you need to promote it.**

LAYING A STRONG FOUNDATION WITH THE PLANNING AND PROMOTION FOR THE PUBLISHING OF YOUR BUSINESS BOOK (PART II)

PROMOTING IT

Think of *"Announcing It"* as a one-time promotion because it is.

Think of *"PROMOTING IT"* as ongoing. You can call it *"Advertising,"* *"Marketing,"* or *"Talking About It."* Call it whatever you want. Just make sure you're selling it!

Accounts you will need to set up for proper promotion and lead generation—*if you don't have them, or another comparable, already:*

- **AWeber Account or ActiveCampaign Account—** *Ideally, use an email account with your domain name.*

AWeber or ActiveCampaign will both leverage all of your list-building efforts. ActiveCampaign has advanced features that may make sense for you, depending on your business goals.

- **<u>Vimeo Account</u>:**

Vimeo will leverage all of your videos on your book landing page, your official expert/authority website, and your training portal for YOUR new training program—*should you desire.*

- **<u>Wistia Account</u>:**

Wistia will leverage all your videos in your Fast Track & Strategic Funnels

- **YouTube<u> Account</u>:**

YouTube will leverage all your social sharing video efforts

- **<u>Facebook Public Figure</u> Page**

Facebook Public Figure Page will leverage your online PR and be your headquarters.

- **RescueTime**

Use this to track your time, and stay focused

Q: When do you have to make a big bold announcement?

A: *Day 1! but no less than 30 days out from launch at the latest—in nine out of ten cases.*

Here's the fun again, Don only had twenty-two days from when he even asked me. It was an early evening call since that's what I scheduled, being that we're in two different time zones. For the sake of argument, he had twenty-one full days. Guess how long we promoted the launch? You guessed it, twenty-one days. It worked well, as it always does.

One enhancement I made to my method, as further leveraging time, a few years ago, I decided: *"Day 1, Week 1."*

Let's be honest, if you have no idea what the process is, you're going to believe anything I tell you, and if it's Day 1, Week 2, 3, 4, 5, 6, or 7—*that's the process.* The same is true for YOUR process and readers.

Once I realized it was in our author's best interest to do it sooner, I quickly wrapped my head around it and changed it. Now between Day 1, Week 1, and Day 1, Week 2 is the norm, on occasion Day 1 Week 3, but always for a while now, well before even the 30-Day mark. Remember that with your readers for your process. Have it make sense–*and follow a real-life calendar*–but don't be afraid to expand and enhance it as time goes on.

Q: What's the difference? How do you decide?

A: *Great question, thanks for asking. It is YOU.*

Some authors want to at least have a title and subtitle before saying anything.

Others want the cover design, and a lot of the writing, justifying there is more validity if you have three chapters written versus one. This is just some internal voice creeping up the same way. Having a third variation of the cover is better than a second variation or refining the title a little bit more. I get it; I'm not going to argue week one. If you don't want to, cool, but you better believe that before day thirty, I will be making the announcement and tagging you on social if you haven't already done so.

I prevent this in 99% of instances by having an application-only process, allowing only the best-of-the-best, fast, imperfect action takers with heart, in my program.

All YOU really need to do is:

- **Have all the expertise from your head, out of it, onto your manuscript**

Promotion is the fun part; it's why I've always loved business, sales, and marketing, it's a creative medium with a point, and you can measure results in profits. Ultimately, sales is serving.

"Selling to me is really serving someone by solving a problem they're begging to have fixed."

~ Mario Fachini

COVER DESIGN *(PART I)*

MOCKUP

There is also this magical thing called *"Photoshop"* that you can grab a rectangle canvas, add some text and color to it, and voila, you have a mock-up of a cover design that you can, and should, share with the world.

Make an announcement that on _____ date, you are launching your book on the topic of _____. You don't even need a name, but if you do, all the better. This is how you first start gauging interest, feedback, and also perhaps begin picking up new clients, speaking engagements, and prospects. Obviously, this will vary, but it's very common for our authors to get leads and start seeing the magic happen even before launch.

PRE-SALES

You will get pre-sales when you implement the **Expert Authority Effect™ Publishing Method.** Most other publishers, regardless of traditional, self, or anything else, make you wait. Why? We're talking about business, and if you can serve, all you need is that person to serve, and a way for them to invest.

I want to be abundantly clear that this is just the testbed for what WILL BE your cover design. Obviously, the better it looks, with proven professional graphic design standards, the better the response it will receive, but remember, working on it forever and never announcing it is horrible. Don't do it. Go to the 80% and be happy. It's not going to print yet. We still have time. All I said was:

ANNOUNCE IT

I have never once in nearly a decade of publishing had any authors comments be:

"You know the post today on LinkedIn @ 3:42 pm looks a lot different than your 2:23 pm post Tuesday on Facebook. Is this a different book?"

They are almost always some variation of:

"That's fantastic!"
"That's wonderful!"
"Congratulations!"
and the always inspiring,

"Where can I get my copy?"

"Promote the heck out of it, and have a way to pay."

~ Mario Fachini

I advise:

www.Square.com or a Wordpress WooCommerce store powered by www.Stripe.com

They're simple, easy, they work. Are they the only games in town? Of course not. If you already have something, use that.

Once you have your store created, take the mock-up image and use it here also. Create an item in the store, test the link to make sure it works 1000% on phones, tablets, desktops, laptops, etc. Have your team test the link out. You can also ask those close to you. The majority will want to support you and invest in the book for real. Either way, test, test, test.

Once you know it's working 150%, promote, promote, promote. Another rule of mine is:

"PERMISSION-BASED" MARKETING ONLY

DO NOT SPAM THE LINK! Talk about the book, share the benefits of the book and get people to ASK YOU for it. NOW you have an opportunity to private message, text, and email them, but **NEVER SPAM IT!**

Add value to the post. Mention you're launching, and share the link with those who ask—*privately in the DMs.* Thank everyone else for their comments.

There will be people who you notice ALWAYS comment but never ask, and it could be a few days to a week or two. I don't have a 1-2-3 solution for those situations, but you will know them when you see them. You can always privately reach out and say, *"I wanted to thank you for your continued support. Were you looking to get a copy of my book?"*

Again, a good portion will say, *"Yeah, absolutely!"* At that point, you can say something like, *"Great, here's the link."* DO NOT go from personable in public to pestering privately, saying, *"I noticed you commenting a lot; here's a link to buy the book."*

PERMISSION-BASED MARKETING

If they don't ask, you don't share—*right out of the gate.*

If you think they want to ask but haven't, YOU ASK. Wait for their response, and *then* potentially share.

You're here to serve them and add value. Always ask first if you don't know.

Finally, always track your progress and sales. If you don't already have a Client Relationship Management software (CRM), I advise Pipedrive–*www.ExpertAuthorityEffect.com/Pipedrive–to keep your progress and sales separated and straightforward.*

Now that we've fully circled the block, we're going back to the cover design.

COVER DESIGN *(PART II)*

Now it's getting serious. Once you start down this path, it becomes real. For most authors, once they see the cover, it becomes more believable. That's why we created the mock-up. It will serve you well to get the ball rolling and momentum, but you will never want only one variation the first time you tried it as the final cover. That is where the cover design Part II comes in, and while we're being honest, part—*or variation three, four, and five-plus.*

AUTHOR BIO

Keep it classy. This is another linchpin, and it can make it or break it. Every part matters: position, credibility, qualifications, third party testimony, brief personal insight, call to action (CTA), etc.

DESCRIPTION

This is do-or-die time. It is essential, not just for ON the book, but for promoting it as well. Amazon doesn't like bad book descriptions, neither do your prospects. They'll both penalize you.

Your book description is one of the best sellers in your author salesforce! Once you have the prospect's attention with the cover design, keep it with the title and subtitle, your book description will go to work for you to close the sale.

WRITING BOOK DESCRIPTIONS THAT SELL

You will want to include:

- Hook
- Benefits
- Pleasure
- Pain
- Positioning-*Why should I listen to you?*
- CTA
- Open Loop

Professional Author Photo

Q: *"What do I want to convey to you?"*

A: *"What do you want to convey, AND how do you want to be positioned?"*

Think about what would, of course, not only look good but also be brand representative, AND positions you congruently with what you would like to convey, as well as relate to who you would like to attract.

Your author photo can make or break the entire book. Every single step we've taken to get here has been first class. Don't drop the ball with a junk photo you expect to pass off as an **Expert Authority Effect™** author photo. Your prospects will see right through it, and you'll be toast.

FRONT

- **Name and title**
- **Bold text**
- **Use bright colors**
- **Easy to read**
- **Image Optional**
- **Be CLEAR with the message you want to convey, if using imagery**
- **Avoid stock photography at nearly all costs. Imagine it shrunken down to the size of a postage stamp**

BACK

The only requirement is really the ISBN. The rest is really what best aligns with your goals. For your consideration:

- **Book description**
- **Benefits of reading the book**
- **About the author**
- **Author photo**
- **Author bio**
- **ISBN**
- **Bar code**
- **CTA**

CASE JACKET CAVEAT

Whether you choose to add more info about you, perhaps your photo on the back, or don't because you feel it's too tight. I get it. I've done multiple books with a non-case jacket back cover design. I have also done multiple books with case jacket back cover design, and will say it's my new preference, it's more professional, I advise it, and you have more space to fit all the authority building goodness you surely have!

This will ALL be changing, nearly daily, for four to five weeks, perhaps six. If we don't end up with more than twenty variations, we haven't refined it enough. Get comfortable knowing it's all a process and might make you uncomfortable.

Even after you think you're finished, there is almost always something you can initially find to make the slightest change on before you print—*especially when it comes to the cover.* You want it to be *"pixel-perfect"* not *"looks pretty good."* This is where I'm blessed to have **The Expert Authority Effect™ Publishing Team** unleash their expertise because you might not notice it—*but the machine it's printed on doesn't care about these details.* Your prospects, however, most certainly will.

No matter what or who you choose, don't skimp on a great cover design, and that includes the back. You should be able to simultaneously work on the front and back cover designs, having the front and back work together as one seamless piece of art. This is ESPECIALLY true when we're talking about your hardcover with a case jacket design. That's 150% the size of a typical book. I invite you to look at what I did on the hardcover version of this book for the case jacket. Let me know when you see it.

A final tip on front and back cover design: often the front and the back look good individually, but if you were to take a scalpel from the back cover to the front cover sideways, edge to edge, it may reveal the text, graphics, and images that are misaligned from the front to the back. Have your graphic designer double-check this so that each section can stand independently on it's own, as well as the whole.

It's a hard thing to catch if you haven't been professionally trained, but your eye see all. It's truthfully a professional photography strategy that dates back to Van Gogh in his famous painting *"Starry Night."* He painted in a way that your eye starts in one spot and travels around the painting, moving closer inward as you go, as always to keep your gaze, taking you deeper and deeper into the artist's world.

Conversely, most graphics nowadays are hacked together by the inexperienced students who learned Photoshop this past weekend. It takes half a second to notice the social media post, website graphic, podcast artwork, YouTube thumbnail, and BOOK COVER. These things are creating confusion in your mind, and worst case, IF they manage to get your attention temporarily, they're directing you right off the screen or page!

Bet Me.

You know you've seen it, that photo that's *"good,"* but you don't understand why you don't *"love it."* Well, my friend, that's why.

I digress, I'm sharing more of the marketing psychology that you can apply to increase the ROI in ALL your marketing—*especially your book*—but we must get back to:

"WRITING IT" SOME MORE

Now that you made the announcement and I gave you a crash course in *"Author Marketing 101,"* let's flip back to the other side of the coin and talk about:

BOOK STRUCTURE

The book structure is the experience you are giving your ideal reader.

This will vary depending on your specific ideal reader, personal and professional goals with the book, and the subject matter expertise.

Below is a sample of some common and widely used book structure elements. I invite you to use them as a palette to drill down the specifics for your book to decide when it's best to use each and why. The main elements in most cases—*for your consideration*—are as follows:

- **PRAISE | REVIEWS | TESTIMONIALS**
- **TITLE PAGE**
- **COPYRIGHT**
- **DEDICATION**
- **CALL TO ACTION (CTA)**
- **CONTENTS | TABLE OF CONTENTS**
- **FOREWARD**
- **PREFACE**
- **PROLOGUE | INTRODUCTION**
- **CHAPTERS 1, 2, 3:**
- 4
- 5
- 6
- 7

- CONCLUSION
- A GIFT FOR YOU
- EPILOGUE | AFTERWARD
- ABOUT THE AUTHOR
- OTHER BOOKS BY THE AUTHOR
- RECOMMENDED READING | READING LIST
- ACKNOWLEDGMENTS
- ENDNOTES
- INDEX
- GLOSSARY
- BONUS
- RESOURCES | CONTACT
- PARTNERS | SPONSORS
- THANK YOU | ASK

Additional Elements for Structure Consideration for Your Business Book:

THE APPENDIX

This allows for the opportunity to share additional information with your reader you may not have covered in the content.

BIBLIOGRAPHY

A list of anything and everything you researched for your book, whether you used–*and cited*–it or not.

REFERENCES AND WORKS CITED

They're pretty much the same thing. Here you only cite what you referenced.

FOOTNOTES

Similar to endnotes but placed at the bottom of the page that contains the referenced sentence versus the end of the book.

YOU'VE DONE IT! CONGRATULATIONS!
No matter how you started, you finished strong!

Now that you have the book written and finalized a rough draft, let's keep moving along to the next step and start editing.

Keep promoting, keep following up for presales EVERY DAY! Track your progress and sales in Pipedrive.

EDITING

The editing process can begin once your manuscript is finished.

Straight up, editing can be a nightmare if it's not one of your core competencies, let alone strengths, but there is a huge opportunity here as well. I invite you into the process. If I can do it, trust me, you will excel! If you're anything like me, you'd rather go speak to 1,000 or 10,000 people for an hour or so, talk to the people afterward, and help them achieve their goal with your unique talent and ability.

I have changed 180° in this area, and that's why I created the:

EXPERT AUTHORITY EFFECT™ HAWKEYE 12 STEP EDITING PROCESS

This combines the use of AI, and no less than three humans on **The Expert Authority Effect™ Publishing Team** to review every word, paragraph, and sentence manually in your manuscript. Making sure your prose is polished and nothing is needed in your narrative.

"Editing your book can be your greatest tool."

~ Mario Fachini

If this is obsessive and overkill, by most standards, it probably is. Remember, it takes six months to build a Rolls Royce and thirteen hours to build a Toyota. The difference is in the care and attention to detail, you deserve the best, and that's what you're getting with us.

This is the **Expert Authority Effect™ Publishing Method!** Not the *"A monkey wrote this with a crayon"* publishing method.

I am beyond blessed to have my family, friends, readers, clients, and the team at **Expert Authority Effect™ Publishing** because the truth is that I failed English seven times. The fact that I have one book, let alone this will be my fifth, is nothing short of a miracle.

While you and I will always take to the stage without hesitation, if you have the slightest inkling to skip the editing stage or rubber stamp it, I implore you not to, and here's why:

I'm imagining you right now, but I want you to imagine YOUR ideal reader. Now imagine they just got done listening, loved your speech, your product, and everything about you in person. What's next? Of course! They want to go deeper, so they get your book in their hands, and that expert authority positioning is shattered by your words on the page.

Unfortunately, people judge and might think you're not smart or that you are lazy, and that's the opposite of what we want. The VERY LEAST you could have done is run a spell check in Word. Even if you stopped there, it would be better than most things that get published– ***BUT PLEASE DON'T STOP THERE***–I'm just saying.

So, to any and everyone who has brought this up to me, while I know I've fought it, **I THANK YOU**, and now I know my readers and their audience will thank you also.

Don't spend a year on this, but don't skip it either. That's why we're not going to skip it. It's time to:

Sharpen Your Writing!

This is a fun section for me because I know there will be at least one person who will think:

"HE...talked about THAT!?"

It reminds me of the image of the caterpillar and butterfly having lunch together. The caterpillar says, *"You've changed,"* and the butterfly says, *"We're supposed to."*

I already told you I changed 180°, and I invite you to join me.

I hear A LOT of people say, *"I have excellent grammar and punctuation."* Well, good for them.

People also say, *"I'm a great editor; I always got the highest marks on my papers,"* or *"I never use spell check, I don't need to, I edit as a write."*

I don't advise this AT ALL. It is one of the worst things you can do to **GET THE BOOK COMPLETED** and in the hands of your prospects.

Let's take this a step further. Let's look at this as a game of poker, and I'll call the edits of your grammar, punctuation, and every last comma and period without missing a single beat, and raise you:

Grammar, punctuation, sentence structure, plagiarism, style, vocabulary enhancement, contextual spelling, proper capitalization, persuasive sales, copywriting, citing your references, and having the finesse, restraint, and discipline to fight your urge to make the author go from a human with emotions, who knows how to connect with the reader, both on and off the page, to sounding like a robot from 1640's England. Having this in your wheelhouse is a clear advantage I didn't start with.

But wait, there's more!

Tautology, ellipsis, sentence structure, fragments, repetitive phrasing, misuse of words, vocabulary enhancement, antecedent, etc.

This section alone could have an entire book on it—*that's not the purpose of why I wrote this one, however.* Here are some examples to get you started:

Tautology | expressing the same information twice.

Example:

"Even though the CEO thought it was necessary, the team felt as if the weekly meeting was Deja vu, all over again."

Proper subjects, hyphens, commas, ending sentences with a preposition, monotonous passages, verbs, nouns, adjectives, forms, past and present tense, missing words, vagueness, intensifiers, and modifiers. All of these often require changing the wording and even rewriting sentences.

Once the writing is complete, the editing is just getting started, and to do it properly; it will take multiple rounds of revisions.

While deep diving on each of these would triple the length of the book and isn't the intent, I want you to realize the importance of every single word you pen and what they can mean, especially on a global scale. I do, however, want to leave you with arguably one of the most critical areas to consider:

Grammatical Voice |

There are multiple grammatical voices:

Passive

Here are examples of passive voice: Our new team has *"been trained,"* or be prepared, is designed, be passed, is transferred, are observed, be removed, be cut off, are designed, be provided, be sent, etc.

Passive: The CEO was informed of the accounting errors.
Active: Mr. Jones informed the CEO of the accounting errors.

Active

Active voice is our goal when writing business books.

Speak in the decisive affirmative, with confidence; you're the expert and authority. *You have mastered your subject matter. You should sound like it.*

This does not mean you should sound like a training manual, operating system, or ignition sequence. Keep that in mind for your final draft. *You must be you, but be the best version of you possible.*

At **Expert Authority Effect™ Publishing**, my team and I make sure all of the content is at the highest level while preserving your voice, even if that means breaking some rules and going against the grain so that you can maintain your confidence from the stage to your team, through your book, and to your ideal reader.

I mean, hey, we didn't get to where we are without breaking some of the rules, some of the time—*did we?*

Plagiarism

Don't do it.

Even if you get flagged, use common sense. I cringe when I see it flagged. Getting flagged for borrowing your own content is hilarious and allowed, as well as encouraged.

Here are a few of the minor areas **The Expert Authority Effect™ Publishing Method** was flagged for:

"There are what seems like endless possibilities."
(You will see soon enough under "Paperback Cover Finish")

Flagged for the text:

https://www.motortrend.com/cars/honda/element/2003/honda-element-suzuki-aerio-sx/

I assure you I didn't stop the momentum I had creating this epic content for you to randomly draw up a web page, spin the wheel, and go:

"Eureka! No one will notice if I use these seven words from a car article."

1.   **Honda wouldn't be my first choice**

2.   **As much as I like cars and MotorTrend, it wouldn't be an automotive website**

3.   **I went to delete and rewrite, but it's so ridiculous and hilarious to me. I figured I'd leave it in so you could have a laugh as well.**

Also, my own Amazon bio:

www.ExpertAuthorityEffect.com/AmazonBio

Depending on when you read this, the *"About the Author"* in the back may or may not match the web page. I did find it quite humorous and I wanted to share with you:

DON'T DO IT!

If you can get flagged for something as ridiculous as your own bio already on the web, as well as a common phrase on a blog post completely unrelated to your subject matter, you will not get away with it. Period.

Furthermore, all it takes is one person to read it, recognize it, and report it. so again:

DON'T DO IT!

You can't hide from 80 billion-plus web pages. The internet is everywhere.

Use only original thoughts in your book, Agreed?

Words That Will Always Win with the Expert Authority Effect™ Publishing Method

Sales Oriented and Persuasive Copywriting will always win— *when appropriate.* *This is a business book, on publishing business books. If you don't incorporate sales, you won't sell anything.*

There is the *"Spray and Pray"* method–*which most amateurs try to use* –and there is the *"Elegant"* way, which I advise you to use, as we do at **Expert Authority Effect™ Publishing.**

I would also caution you that editing is a craft, and another layer, that could take a year to start understanding, and a lifetime to master.

But don't skip it either.

The 5 most persuasive words in the English language:

- **You**
  Right or wrong, there is nothing anyone is more interested in than themselves.

- **FREE**
  Everyone loves a good deal, and what's a better deal than this?

- **Instantly**
  Immediate gratification.

- **New:**
  It's called the "*News*," because it is relevant and recent.

- **Because:**
  Because is a simple yet incredibly powerful word BECAUSE it gives someone a reason to do something.

Ellen Langer, a social psychologist and professor at Harvard University, conducted a study in 1978 on the power of the word "*because*." Langer had people ask if they could "*cut in line*" waiting for the copy machine—*this was before PCs and printers became so popular.*

The researchers gave the people three different phrases to use to get permission to cut into the line. Each phrase was specifically worded as follows:

- **"Excuse me; I have 5 pages. May I use the Xerox™ machine?"**

- **"Excuse me; I have 5 pages. May I use the Xerox™ machine, because I have to make copies?"**

- **"Excuse me; I have 5 pages. May I use the Xerox™ machine, because I'm in a rush?"**

Which one do you think worked best? I'll wait.

*** *Cue Jeopardy Theme Song* ***

Got it? Good, here are the results:

- *"Excuse me; I have 5 pages. May I use the Xerox™ machine?"*: **60% compliance**

- *"Excuse me; I have 5 pages. May I use the Xerox™ machine, because I have to make copies?"*: **93% compliance**

- *"Excuse me; I have 5 pages. May I use the Xerox™ machine, because I'm in a rush?"*: **94% compliance**

Something as simple as making a copy can still have a dramatic increase in desired results from one simple word:

"Because."

The kicker to me is that the reasons aren't even that great! There was only a *1% difference* in compliance between *"because I have to make copies,"* and a semi-more reasonable expectation *"because I'm in a rush."*

Want to have some fun?
Imagine saying this at your office, or your client's office:
"because I don't want to wait."

Let me know how it works. I'm sure you'll get 100% compliance since it's your office. No matter where you try it next, remember it's simple words that make a significant difference.

At **Expert Authority Effect™ Publishing**, we leverage more than 500 plus specific words, grammar, and formatting, strategically as a part of our **Expert Authority Effect™ HawkEye 12 Step Editing Process** to ensure your business book is truly in league with not only being well written, but generating leads and profits.

I'm not writing a book on copywriting and persuasive selling. I simply want you to realize it's not just your social media posts, emails, sales letters, videos, podcasts, marketing, and advertising. *It's EVERYWHERE!, 24/7, ALL THE TIME!*

What I'm sharing with you is one of the many fundamental differences with what we do. I've taught this specific subject to countless entrepreneurs to help them improve their marketing. Along with my **Expert Authority Effect™ Messaging Training Program** I mentioned earlier.

I want to reiterate this point as it's paramount to your success both inside and outside of your book. Alright, you talked me into it! Here are a few more examples:

"When"

You wouldn't think it's a big deal, but it's one of the most common things I see in entrepreneurs' copy that have come to me for consulting.

Watch how powerful a few simple words can be:

"When" versus *"If"*

~~"If you'd like to give us a call to get started,"~~
"When you give us a call to get started."

Which one do you think converts higher and increases the rate of calls your business will receive?

SIMPLY, EASILY, AS LOW AS, ONLY, AND IMAGINE

Imagine never having to guess why your online ads aren't converting as well as you hoped.

Imagine the joy of easily increasing your email open rate AND click-thru rate.

Imagine knowing there is no difference in the manufacturing cost of a $10 bill to a $20 bill.

Imagine knowing the proper words to use in all instances to convert your $1 bills to $100 bills.

Simply knowing, the only difference is the messaging on the front of the bill.

If ever there is a place you want to get these words right, it's your business book. Now, with all the cards on the table, do you still want to make that bet?

In those famous words portrayed by Tom Hanks:

"...and that's all I have to say about that!"

~ Forest Gump

FORMATTING

PRINT INTERIOR

Margins, Typography, Fonts, Bullets, Bold, Spacing, Tracking, Kerning, Titles, Tables, Images, Quotes, Headers, Footers & Trim Size, *Oh My!*

This is way up there with editing. The reality is, again, this more than likely isn't your area of expertise–*nor is it really mine*–but I've learned a thing or two over the last decade, and I'll give you a quick rundown. By no means is this a full and exhaustive list of all you can use in your arsenal. I want to discuss some of the most common formatting issues and decisions I have incorporated with each new book I publish.

Margins | Make effective use of margins; I remember in all of my art classes learning about *"negative space"* the space around and between the subject in a piece of art or a photograph. The principle is the same in a book. The challenge is for the words to flow well on the page, and look elegant while they are being read—*not a jumbled mess.*

Typography | In short, it is *"the design within the design."* You can have the best content in the world, but if it isn't legible, readable, and enjoyable to your reader, they're not going to get through it. It's also the one class in college–*the days I was there*–that I always wanted to take but didn't have the opportunity before I left. It fascinated me. I'm not going to go off on an art and creative studies tangent, but I want you to consider it because the use of type is another way to make a good book, great.

Fonts | Fonts aren't your friend when you're working on the content of your book. The fonts aren't the focus, nor is their size; the focus is your expertise on the paper. Now that we're formatting, fonts are your best friend and will only enhance great content with the right ones but can also downgrade your content if you choose the wrong ones.

Font's will also change the number of pages in your book, even if the font size is the same. Font size will change the page count a lot as well, in addition to the spacing, indenting, and the overall experience for your reader.

You will want to decide between a serif font and a sans serif font. **Since we're focusing on your nonfiction business book, I would suggest that you use a serif font since it enhances the readability of your book.**

Font size will vary, not only in your book, but also in your preference, and what supports your body of work the best. You may prefer smaller, or larger, and that is 100% your decision. **I will say again to keep in mind first and foremost your ideal reader's preference, who they are, and how long you expect them to be reading.**

I gravitate to making life easier rather than harder, so I tend to use, and advise, 12pt to 14pt font. We're writing a business book for your ideal prospects with the intent of adding value by helping them solve their biggest problem; we want them to get through the entire thing AND act by implementing what they just learned. Use this book as an example and tell me, are you happier with me? This font is larger, or would you rather it be a lot smaller?—*You're welcome.*

Keep your ideal reader's experience in mind as you write your book. Let's continue to:

Bullets | Wow, I just thought of *"numbered lists,"* and below the *"Bold,"* should I give an honorable mention to *Italic* and <u>Underline</u>? Do you see how staggering this becomes? From my view, it isn't adding a lot to the bottom line, as far as getting your book out there and into someone's hands, to get them the result they desire that you can give them right now? I'd be hard-pressed to believe someone would read this book, put it into action, and another person would be so offended by a line break, bold, pipe, or numbered list when it should be bulleted, they'd stop reading in protest and never follow through, moreover, is this really the ideal reader, prospect, and client you're looking to attract? Left alignment, center, right alignment, and justify popped in my head. Dad always used justify in his business for survey reports. I like to justify when appropriate, for this reason. I love & miss you, Dad.

- **Use bullet points for lists of items**
- **Don't have them all bunched up in a paragraph**
- **Remember your ideal reader must get through the book**
- **I still don't know when you would use #'s instead**
- **I'm sure my team will tell, and take care of it for us**

Bold | It has it's place, and as you can see, the main thought is in bold. As I look at it now, both *"Margins"* and *"Typography"* are **BOLD**, and on *"margins,"* I have the bullet point as well.

Margins | We'll see where it ends up by the time you read this, I will keep it bold, but I think the bullet points aren't also needed. What's the official rule? When do you do what? I have no idea. As I mentioned, I would defer to my **World Class Expert Authority Effect™ Publishing Team**. Sometimes it just comes down to what *"looks good,"* for example sake, let's leave them in here.

As far as the | Pipes | are concerned, I went through and added them to everything—*I actually really like it.* It looks great (IMHO). Is it breaking some rule? The sheer fact that I did it tells me eighty plus percent, *"Yes."*

I think I'm going to keep them. They look terrific. I have to thank one of my author clients, who I mentioned earlier, Rocio Perez, who was reviewing a webpage on *www.EAInterviews.com*, when I was launching my show in early 2019, around the same time we were publishing her first book, she mentioned the "-" makes people think *"negative,"* so we got rid of every single line break on the page and it really classed it up. Thanks, Rocio!

Spacing | Spacing is also known as leading, and it can be one of your greatest assets as it allows for a smooth transition of the sentences to flow into paragraphs and paragraphs to flow into pages. Whether you've noticed or not, reading up to this point, the result I wanted you to experience was deliberate. Too much spacing and you lose the energy and momentum, too little spacing, or improperly done spacing, and you have 40,000 words of alphabet soup. *You always want to strive for the best balance for your ideal reader's experience.*

Tracking | While spacing refers to the overall aesthetic as a whole, tracking is specific to the uniform spacing over a range of characters. It might not be the entire book or even a chapter; it could just be the paragraph at the end of the chapter, or most likely, the end paragraph on the back cover design.

Kerning | Let's take it down one more notch. If you've enjoyed spacing and tracking, kerning is going to be the cherry on top—*or should I say, in between.* Kerning gets down to the nitty-gritty and allows you to adjust the spacing in between letters on the character level. The magic you can do with kerning is unparalleled for the overall aesthetic. Done properly, it's beautiful.

Leading | While tracking and kerning deal with the horizontal spacing between either the group of letters or the characters themselves, *respectively,* leading is the vertical spacing between the line of text.

Titles | Straightforward yet essential, the titles let your ideal reader know the beginning–*and consequently the ending*–of each chapter, so they know where they are in your book, and give them an immediate preview for what they are about to learn.

Tables | You may or may not have tables in your business book, but they are an important consideration. If you use them, you want them presented legibly, clearly, and appropriately sized when you are showcasing information that is best suited for tables.

Images | You may or may not have images in your business book; if you decide to use them, you will want the highest resolution. This means 300 dots per inch (DPI) or higher since it has to look great for not only Kindle/eBook but also print. You don't have the forgiveness of a website on your side here. You may recall the image of the napkin earlier for my VIP Book Launch and Awards Ceremony LIVE! Event. You may have also noticed I don't have 50 plus images per chapter. Again this is intentional.

A picture is worth 1,000 words, but 25-30 images alone won't make your book. Adding too many, however, can be problematic in achieving the desired experience and consistency throughout it. Don't be shy. Add when appropriate, but I'd advise using sparingly. Lastly, consider if the image can and will lend itself well to black and white print, or does it NEED to be in color.

If the image will add value, great, go for it, but don't run this risk of making a formatting nightmare simply because you want to look fancy. Remember, your book is simply the beginning of the journey. Your ideal reader—*and prospect,* will end up on your websites and social anyhow. K.I.S.S. Remember, it's a business book focus, not a children's book.

Quotes | Quotes are an excellent way to bring depth to your business book in a condensed form. They strengthen your position on your subject matter. You can add further authority and credibility by using your own or contextual depth by quoting others. They are often used to kick off a new chapter as a teaser for what the chapter contains. You have read examples from the start of this book, and they will continue for all the reasons mentioned above. *While not required, I'd encourage them, but don't go overboard. Again, K.I.S.S. There is eloquence in brevity.*

Headers | Headers are the beauty above the beauty. Headers are a great way to personalize your business book further, make it your own, as well as enhance your ideal reader's experience, provide further information and reinforcement for the book, author, and subject matter.

Footers | Footers are the beauty below the beauty. Footers are another way to personalize your business book further and achieve your desired experience for your ideal reader; you will want to remember to include the page numbers, as most books have them somewhere at the bottom. I have seen some at the top, but it is less common. You can do what you want—*as this is your business book*—but don't go so far off the reservation that it doesn't make sense to your ideal reader, or at the very least, they have to question it. *Take everything into account for the final design before you go to print. The juice may not be worth the squeeze.*

Trim Size | Remember me teasing you in chapter one? Here is the final answer again for your notes: "*6 x 9.*" One reason why is that it's a standard size and works well, but also one of my favorite author's, Robert Kiyosaki, talked about it in over a dozen of his books. Using "*6 x 9*" allows people to turn it sideways to make a copy. You might have already done this with mine. If so, you're welcome. If not, give it a shot. I thought this was a cool idea, again, yours is a business book, not Harry Potter.

Also, it's larger, and like I just mentioned, I gravitate to a larger font, as you want your reader to have their most enjoyable experience.

KINDLE VS PRINT

They might be the same book, but Kindle/eBook are not formatted the same as printed books.

The biggest difference between the two is "*static,*" versus "*dynamic*" text—*where the paper won't change size on you, but the zoom on your electronic device will.*

Additionally, you must deal with reflowable text—*think in terms of "responsive web design."* If you're not familiar with either, it's industry-specific fancy talk that simply means: *the text size and layout will 100% vary by device.*

Kindle/eBook Specifics:

- **No blank pages**

- **No page numbers**

- **Dynamic text size**
  (device dependent)

- **Dynamic visible content on the page**
  (screen size dependent)

- **Images will render** *(appear)* **differently across devices**

- **Tables/Charts/Graphs are susceptible to dynamic sizing**

- **Overall, there are a lot of uncontrollable variances, and you can't compensate for it 100%.** *Be comfortable with this. It's okay. Focus on the best content you can.*

The Expert Authority Effect™ Publishing Method is the first book I even added substantial images to for this exact reason. In my experience, I'd advise you to avoid it as much as you can. If you do add these elements, realize they can vary greatly. DO NOT go overboard with them; they can become another nightmare area—*as I've mentioned,* and it just brings you another foot closer to getting stuck in the rabbit hole.

Some Other Cool Features Specific to Kindle/eBook

- **Hyperlinks can be added and actually linked**
  (www.ExpertAuthorityEffect.com) has been mentioned throughout the book as well as
  www.EAInterviews.com on the previous pages. Think *"webpage"* when you think Kindle/eBook. While technically it's not, the functionality and experience are very similar.

This is why you've seen the: *(www.ExpertAuthorityEffect.com/ LinkJustMentioned) style* throughout the book, so you can take advantage of checking out the site and learning more, but also not getting lost in a sea of weird-looking domain names and extensions. While on Kindle/ eBook, it wouldn't matter since any word can be linked. When you read this in print, I also wanted to have the URL make sense and be memorable for you.

- **Book Lending can enable the ability for someone to "lend" the book to someone digitally. I think that's cool; I've done it, at some point, with all of mine.**

Q: "Does that mean you don't get paid since they didn't buy it?!"

A: *"Kinda" You receive a smaller royalty, based or how much of the book they read. For all intents and purposes, however, you don't get paid the full amount, but who cares!*

So someone wants to learn what you have to say on the topic? Then say, *Heck yeah, here's a copy, glad I can help. Enjoy!"*

*Expert Authority Effect™ Purpose Time still: Why would you squabble over AT MOST a $9.99 Kindle that you're only getting 70% of anyways? $7 versus—*what's that new client worth to you again from Chapter 1?*

Every New Client is Worth $ _____ to Me *(fill in the blank)*

FORGIVENESS & EASE TO UPDATE

Do you know what's great about digital documents? They're just text, which is very quick and easy to update, just like a website. While you can't—*unfortunately*—log in to Amazon, open a text editor to change what you want, and click *"save"*—or *"publish"* like WordPress, you CAN open, update the finalized document—*albeit Word, or InDesign*, click save, and re-upload it to Kindle. Then you let the process begin again, and voila, once it's done, it's live again—*no need to worry about 100,000 copies of your book that you wanted to reword quickly.* You can go ahead and enhance your manuscript as you see fit—*which comes in handy as things change over time between your re-launches.*

No matter the reason why you want to make a change, smile, and be excited, that you can, and it's way easier than:

PRINT

Yeah, not so much. If it's printed wrong, it's printed wrong. That's why I created the: **Expert Authority Effect™ HawkEye 12 Step Editing Process** for all our authors. To mitigate this from happening the first time around, and if some small thing does slip by, we catch it the best we can before printing.

I will share with you a few of the strategies that we use—*that you can use also.* While technically we're not on to publishing and printing yet, we're close enough that I don't want to leave it out.

Go to the Kindle Direct Publishing (KDP) account you setup: *(www.ExpertAuthorityEffect.com/KDP)* and simply:

Order Author Copies first–*up to five*–*and have them PHYSICALLY looked over before you approve them to go to a full run print production.* The text might appear harder to read than you thought, your author image is darker than you anticipated, the front cover image–*if it includes a photo*–may look different than the screen, the binding might not be as thick as you had hoped, etc. No matter the *"what,"* just know, while it's not anyone's desire to have mistakes, or more work, but what an opportunity, however, it is to be able to refine it with minimal effort, or without signing over a higher percentage of royalties, part of the company, or having to wait until the next quarter or year! Simply invest in a few more copies of the book plus nominal shipping and handling, and you can refine it further—*and just because a book is from a "traditional publisher" doesn't mean it's immune from imperfections. There are plenty of big-name author's books out there that weren't done perfectly.*

Do a small batch first run print. Once you approve the author copies, do a small run of 25 to 100 copies. While you want them to be perfect the first time–*and that's possible*–*you may have added "just a little more" to the chapter, which in turn added some extra pages or affected the formatting.* Now the book is literally 1/16 to 1/8 of an inch thicker. The added thickness can affect the pixel-perfect binding measurement you had already dialed in and looked great on screen, printed just *"off enough"* that you *"like it"* but don't *"love it."* Almost no one will notice, but it might drive you nuts, and you don't want that to happen.

In conclusion, formatting is often called: *Interior Book Design, Layout, Layout Design, or Book Layout.*

Even if this is your skillset, in this instance, you're the author. I'd advise you have another professional commit to this responsibility. if you don't have someone on your team, you may consider:

- Fiverr: www.ExpertAuthorityEffect.com/Fiverr
- Upwork: www.ExpertAuthorityEffect.com/Upwork
- Vellum: www.ExpertAuthorityEffect.com/Vellum
- Atticus: www.ExpertAuthorityEffect.com/Atticus
- 99Designs: www.ExpertAuthorityEffect.com/99Designs
- BookBaby: www.ExpertAuthorityEffect.com/BookBaby

There are many other options, but this is a good start for you. Your goal is to extract your expertise, then further finesse and refinement before going down this rabbit hole. I know, however, that curiosity, or you're actually on this step, will happen either way, so I hope this helps.

As with many others, Fiverr and Upwork, have people that can do it, Vellum is software similar to Atticus—*but MAC only*, 99Designs, and BookBaby are higher-end service-based options that you won't need to *"dig"* for the right person. To this day, I have never attempted this on my own books, and I don't advise you to either.

While I know, there are qualified people through the resources listed above, I am thankful I don't have to spend my time shopping around since I have the world-class **Expert Authority Effect™ Publishing Team** so that I can focus on YOUR results, the way you should not worry about this, and stay focused on YOUR ideal reader's results.

No matter what you decide is right for you and your book, make sure the result is something you will not only be proud of but always excited to share with the world.

This feels like the right place to end this topic and chapter.

Print is different than digital; you've gotten this far, don't slack now, simply because you think you're over the hump. You deserve the best, and so does your ideal reader.

"*Let us read and let us dance; these two amusements will never do any harm to the world.*"

~ *Voltaire*

Publishing

Publishing is where this whole thing comes full circle, and one of the main points is where I believe the magic happens. Anyone can write a social media post. A large portion of entrepreneurs write articles or blogs. You've heard about eBooks, but even with those, I always question *"Kindle"* or *"eBook"* because, for most people, a downloadable PDF is advertised as an *"eBook."—it may or may not be.*

Finishing and formatting your manuscript is one thing and no small feat. While a great start you know we're not stopping at *"Good Enough"* for your final product.

Welcome to the world of–*actually*–publishing!

I am now going to bring you right back to your comfort zone in the top 5-10%, and perhaps, when you stick to the plan, especially in the next chapter on publicity, you'll choose to advance even further to the very top, as we do with our concierge author clients. No matter what you decide to do, we still must actually *"publish"* your book.

We've talked about it numerous times throughout the book already, and publishing is no different.

You're essentially publishing two books:

- **Kindle/eBook**
- **Physical Book** *(Paperback & Hardcover)*

In the strictest sense of the word, once you've uploaded your book to Kindle—*through the Kindle Direct Publishing Platform (KDP) that we set up in Chapter 3: PLAN,* **it is published!**

Exciting right? Of course, there is a waiting period that you will see once you log in to KDP that will say something like, *"It may take up to 72 hours for your book to be published on the platform."*

I'm not going to publish in ink the exact numbers of my combined stats after nearly a decade of publishing, so I'll re-iterate one of my primary messages of this book: **"Allow enough time before launch and follow the game plan I've laid out for you here."**

KINDLE DIRECT PUBLISHING (KDP)

In recent years, Amazon has been enhanced this part, and now you can stay in KDP for both Kindle/eBook as well as the printed version. It's nice and makes sense from a business standpoint as to why they did it.

As I write this, I cannot confirm or deny if I have early access or not, or if they may have a hardcover option in the future, depending on the time you read this, varying from when it was published—*but don't be surprised if one day your dashboard looks like mine.*

Getting physical copies through KDP may or may not be in your best interest, depending on your goals for the final product. Keep reading. More on this soon enough.

You will see two options that say, *"Standard Distribution"* and *"Expanded Distribution."* I will elaborate after the following few main bullet points, but to maximize Amazon as well as all the networks, you will want to choose *"Standard Distribution."* This is STRICTLY for AMAZON's partner distribution network; it doesn't mean anything other than who AMAZON is pushing you out to. There are other, and more profitable ways I advise for expanded distribution. I will cover the areas that require the most detail, and I get the most questions on.

Book Description

Remember that book description we worked on earlier in Chapter 3: PLAN? It's time to put it to use. It's time for it to shine now. You're now welcome to use it for the back cover design of the book. Grab it and add it.

Categories

Think of categories basically as keywords, tags, or #hashtags everywhere else on the internet. Categories get broken down into sub-categories starting with:

- **High-level Categories**
- **Subcategories**
- **Specific categories**
- **Niche categories**
- **Specific niche categories**
- **Super-niche categories**

Here are two that I'm considering for this book. You will see they go 5-6 levels deep.

- Books > Reference > Writing, Research & Publishing Guides > Publishing & Books > Bibliographies & Indexes > Business
- Kindle Store > Kindle eBooks > Reference > Writing, Research & Publishing Guides > Publishing & Books > Authorship

Amazon only allows you to choose two categories through KDP, but—*at the time of this writing*—when you email them, you can add up to eight more.

This is the categories list—*up to two*—directly from KDP:

Amazon (Level I) Categories:

- Fiction
- **Nonfiction** (*select this one*)
- Juvenile Fiction
- Juvenile Nonfiction
- Comics & Graphic Novels
- Education & Reference
- Literary Collections
- Non-Classifiable

Since we're focused on publishing your lead and profit-generating nonfiction business book, I'm going to skip all the rest but know that more exist. I'm sure you're already experiencing how nutty this can quickly get—*and if not, give it a few more pages.* Further caveat and transparency, I'm leaving the subcategories from the 1ˢᵗ edition only—*as an example*–so we both don't lose our minds.

This is something you and your team really should be doing on a computer with a large screen. Even if you're reading this on a kindle, it's nuts. However, I want to illustrate the reality of what's going on, so you're in the best place possible, literally and figuratively, for when you publish. I do, however, ask you to permit me some leniency on truncating the content to fit the book. Thanks in advance.

DEEP BREATH

Here we go!

Nonfiction (Level II) Subcategories:

- Antiques & Collectibles
- Architecture
- Art
- Bibles
- Biography & Autobiography
- Body, Mind & Spirit
- **Business & Economics** *(select this one)*
- Computers
- Cooking
- Crafts & Hobbies
- Design
- Drama
- Family & Relationships
- Games
- Gardening
- Health & Fitness

- History
- House & Home
- Humor
- Language Arts & Disciplines
- Law
- Literary Criticism
- Mathematics
- Medical
- Music
- Nature
- Performing Arts
- Pets
- Philosophy
- Photography
- Poetry
- Political Science
- Psychology
- Religion
- Science
- Self-Help
- Social Science
- Sports & Recreation
- Technology & Engineering
- Transportation
- Travel
- True Crime

It's exciting to think about how in-depth this gets because that's how Amazon ensures your business book will get in the right hands of your ideal prospects.

Below you will quickly see how insane it would be to list all subcategories for a book; it would serve you best to watch our short video on it. Again, I'm not looking to print a ream of paper—*despite having a Dunder Mifflin corporate account,* I do, however, want you to know that this is the reality of publishing, and every single one of these categories goes another 1-2 levels deep.

This is just the surface. As I illustrated above, you see they can go 5-6 levels deep. I just deleted all the subcategories that aren't relevant.

Here is what's important to you: **Business.**

Nonfiction (Level III) Subcategories Expanded

- Antiques & Collectibles
- Architecture
- Art
- Bibles
- Biography & Autobiography
- Body, Mind & Spirit

Business & Economics

- **General**

- **Accounting (Level IV)**
  - **General**
  - **Financial**
  - **Governmental**
  - **Managerial**
  - **Standards**

- **Advertising & Promotion**
- **Auditing**
- **Banks & Banking**
- **Bookkeeping**
- **Budgeting**

- Business Communication (Level IV)
  - General
  - Meetings & Presentations
- Business Ethics
- Business Etiquette
- Business Law
- Business Mathematics
- Business Writing
- Careers (Level IV)
  - General
  - Internships
  - Job Hunting
  - Resumes
- Commerce
- Commercial Policy
- Conflict Resolution & Mediation
- Consulting
- Consumer Behavior
- Corporate & Business History
- Corporate Finance (Level IV)
  - General
  - Private Equity
  - Valuation
  - Venture Capital
- Corporate Governance
- Crowdfunding
- Customer Relations
- Decision-Making & Problem Solving

- Development (Level IV)
  - General
  - Business Development
  - Economic Development
  - Sustainable Development
- Distribution
- E-Commerce (Level IV)
  - General
  - Auctions & Small Business
  - Internet Marketing
  - Online Trading
- Econometrics
- Economic Conditions
- Economic History
- Economics (Level IV)
  - General
  - Comparative
  - Macroeconomics
  - Microeconomics
  - Theory
- Education
- Entrepreneurship
- Environmental Economics
- Exports & Imports
- Facility Management
- Finance (Level IV)
  - General
  - Financial Engineering

- - Financial Risk Management
  - Wealth Management
- Forecasting
- Foreign Exchange
- Franchises
- Free Enterprise
- Government & Business
- Green Business
- Home-Based Businesses
- Human Resources & Personnel Management
- Industrial Management
- Industries (Level IV)
  - General
  - Agribusiness
  - Automobile Industry
  - Computers & Information Technology
  - Energy
  - Entertainment
  - Fashion & Textile Industry
  - Financial Services
  - Food Industry
  - Hospitality, Travel & Tourism
  - Manufacturing
  - Media & Communications
  - Natural Resource Extraction
  - Park & Recreation Management
  - Pharmaceutical & Biotechnology
  - Retailing
  - Service
  - Transportation

- Inflation
- Information Management
- Infrastructure
- Insurance (Level IV)

  - General
  - Automobile
  - Casualty
  - Health
  - Liability
  - Life
  - Property
  - Risk Assessment & Management

- Interest
- International (Level IV)

  - General
  - Accounting
  - Economics
  - Marketing
  - Taxation

- Investments & Securities (Level IV)

  - General
  - Analysis & Trading Strategies
  - Bonds

    - Commodities (Level V)

  - Derivatives
  - Futures
  - Mutual Funds
  - Options

- Portfolio Management
- Real Estate
- Stocks
- Knowledge Capital
- Labor
- Leadership
- Mail Order
- Management
- Management Science
- Marketing (Level IV)

  - General
  - Direct
  - Industrial
  - Multilevel
  - Research
  - Telemarketing

- Mentoring & Coaching
- Mergers & Acquisitions
- Money & Monetary Policy
- Motivational
- Museum Administration & Musicology
- Negotiating
- New Business Enterprises
- Nonprofit Organizations & Charities (Level IV)

  - General
  - Finance & Accounting
  - Fundraising & Grants
  - Management & Leadership
  - Marketing & Communications

- Office Automation
- Office Equipment & Supplies
- Office Management
- Operations Research
- Organizational Behavior
- Organizational Development
- Outsourcing
- Personal Finance (Level IV)

  - General
  - Budgeting
  - Investing
  - Money Management
  - Retirement Planning
  - Taxation

- Personal Success
- Production & Operations Management
- Project Management
- Public Finance
- Public Relations
- Purchasing & Buying
- Quality Control
- Real Estate (Level IV)

  - General
  - Buying & Selling Homes
  - Commercial
  - Mortgages

- Reference
- Research & Development

- **Sales & Selling (Level IV)**
  - General
  - Management

- **Secretarial Aids & Training**
- **Skills**
- **Small Business**
- **Statistics**
- **Strategic Planning**
- **Structural Adjustment**
- **Taxation (Level IV)**

  - General
  - Corporate
  - Small Business

- **Time Management**
- **Total Quality Management**
- **Training**
- **Urban & Regional**
- **Women in Business**
- **Workplace Cultures**

Nonfiction (Level III) Subcategories Continued:

- Computers
- Cooking
- Crafts & Hobbies
- Design
- Drama
- Family & Relationships
- Games
- Gardening
- Health & Fitness

- History
- House & Home
- Humor
- Language Arts & Disciplines
- Law
- Literary Criticism
- Mathematics
- Medical
- Music
- Nature
- Performing Arts
- Pets
- Philosophy
- Photography
- Poetry
- Political Science
- Psychology
- Religion
- Science
- Self-Help
- Social Science
- Sports & Recreation
- Technology & Engineering
- Transportation
- Travel
- True Crime

I don't even know how many subcategories there were in *"Business & Economics"* alone, but I did count 19 level IV and V categories. I doubt you're thinking, *"that's it?"* but I do want to be clear that:

Categories are critical.

With our concierge-level service, We invest a large portion of our time discussing and doing the category research for you because of how involved it is, the impact it can make on your book, who sees it, and most importantly, who doesn't.

Do you want the real kicker? As I'm telling you the importance of drilling down and being super specific for your categories, I just looked and guess what Amazon themselves did?

THE EXACT SAME THING!

Since the 1st edition, the **LEVEL 1** categories have **MORE THAN DOUBLED** and are now as follows:

- **Literature & Fiction**
- **Nonfiction**
- **Romance**
- **Mystery, Thriller & Suspense**
- **Science Fiction & Fantasy**
- **Religion & Spirituality**
- **Health, Fitness & Dieting**
- **Business & Money**
- **Foreign Languages**
- **Politics & Social Sciences**
- **Teen & Young Adult**
- **History**
- **Science & Math**
- **Biographies & Memoirs**
- **Self-Help**
- **Children's Books**
- **LGBTQ+ Books**
- **Computers & Technology**
- **Medical Books**
- **Humor & Entertainment**

- Comics, Manga & Graphic Novels
- Reference
- Education & Teaching
- Parenting & Relationships
- Cookbooks, Food & Wine
- Arts & Photography
- Sports & Outdoors
- Crafts, Hobbies & Home
- Travel
- Law
- Engineering & Transportation

That's just **LEVEL 1 ALONE!**

While we're going to move on and discuss pricing. **DO NOT SKIMP,** shortcut, or blow off this step. I know you want to make an impact and have the most significant reach possible; *your categories are one of the sharpest arrows in your quiver to accomplish your goal.*

Now that we have scratched the surface of categories let's move on to the last few items for your Kindle Business eBook.

PRE-ORDER

"I am ready to release my book now."

This is what we will primarily focus on, even though Amazon has it's own pre-order option. I have heard *dozens* of stories of authors who have done this only to get overwhelmed, never finish the book, then feel worse because they couldn't deliver not only what they started, but have to explain to everyone who already supported them and got a copy. Not to mention, if you DON'T meet the deadline, Amazon will freeze your account, and you won't be able to launch another book for a year!

If you noticed, I already walked you through extracting your expertise on paper, and congrats again for completing it. That was 100% intentional. When I created the **Expert Authority Effect™ Publishing Method**—*and every time I refine it*—I always keep your experience paramount, and it will always be first-class. Amazon's pre-order may be an option for you, but Amazon isn't the only option for generating pre-orders, as we've already covered earlier in the book. I did want to cover this on the chance you do want to make a Wall Street Journal, USA Today, or New York Time's Bestseller run. Having your book available through multiple retailers is one requirement.

Pricing

I've taught 10/20/30 for years and still advise it to get started.
$10 for Kindle
$20 for Softcover
$30 for Hardcover

Keep it simple. Focus your efforts on getting it in people's hands, adding value, and serving them, instead of trying to turn a dime into a dollar.

Start with a $100 bill.

I know, I know...so I'll add this, *"when you're ready for advanced marketing techniques, promotion, and all of this is 150% complete, with your list building underway, audiobook finished, a suite of training available, your own show and thriving YouTube channel, we can talk about price differentials, split testing, ad conversions across different audiences, limited-time promo pricing strategies, tracking and refining your results. I'm skipping it now to keep you focused. Not because it's not possible, K.I.S.S."*

KINDLE/EBOOK

You have two royalty options to choose from: *35% and 70%*

70% Naturally, you'd want 70%. The downside is the range is capped from $2.99 to $9.99. Amazon doesn't want to lose money on the low end by giving you too much of a small amount—*$0.99/$1.99*, so your only option is 35%. Conversely, they don't want to give away the farm to authors with a $100 plus to $200 price for an eBook, so they discourage this by limiting the 70% royalty. The upside is, it's still 70%, and you will generate the most sales in this range anyhow. Don't overthink it, just set it–*at 70%*–and forget it.

35% While much less of a profit margin, you gain more freedom. Amazon allows for a much greater pricing range at 35%. You can choose the 35% royalty option as low a $0.99 all the way up to $200. Amazon's primary focus is to protect their margins, as well as buyers from most people selling $200 Kindle eBooks, even though you can. Amazon knows they will be making the lions share in that scenario.

Stick to the 10/20/30 model for now, and you'll be good. Remember, this is just one more step in the process. Keep it big picture.

PRINT

For print, it changes to 60% and 40%

60% Keep your book on Amazon; you make more, they make more, and everyone wins. Do This.

40% Expanded–*Through Amazon's Distribution Partner Network.*

As I mentioned at the start of this chapter, I'm circling back to it now. One reason we only want *"Standard Distribution"* with the 60% royalty, is the distribution.

The following is directly from Amazon's website:

"Enrolling your paperback in Expanded Distribution doesn't guarantee it will be ordered by a particular bookseller or library. The decision to order your book lies solely with the individual booksellers and libraries. We can't provide details on which booksellers and libraries purchased your book."

The answer is: *"Most won't"*

I have it on very good authority that if you self-publish your book on Amazon, bookstores, booksellers, and libraries flag it and intentionally DON'T pick it up because it's from Amazon.

Moreover, book stores are high overhead businesses with a low-profit margin. If your distributor doesn't offer them a buy-back guarantee— *That is, if your book doesn't sell off the shelf, they can return them for a refund.* I know you'd be shocked to know:

Amazon Doesn't

Amazon wants to sell on Amazon, not take their time, energy, money, and resources promoting third parties. Naturally, they now take an even larger cut—*as if they weren't already getting enough.* Previously, When I published my first book—*which is now a #1 International Best Seller*—**"Video Marketing for Business Owners"** in 2012, the royalties were 70% and 30%—*respectively.* It has changed over the years, and while I hope it at least stays here, it very well may change again, with a slim chance it goes back to Amazon making less.

YOU also want to be able to sell on Amazon, and I don't mean publishing your business book on Amazon. *We're already doing that!* I mean the Amazon Marketing Services (AMS) paid ad system that gives you the opportunity to pay for ads so you can increase the reach and narrow the targeting for the exposure of your book once it's on their platform.

There are people out there teaching to be everywhere else BUT here, because *"Amazon takes too much."* While I'd rather it be 70/30—*and higher*, without a doubt! I'm keeping it big picture. While they argue over who's getting a larger percentage of the dime, I will gladly take the $100 bill. This is where our premier partner BookBaby (*www. ExpertAuthorityEffect.com/BookBaby)*, comes in and will help you with the expanded distribution while keeping your profits the highest they can be.

PRINTING PAPERBACK KINDLE DIRECT PUBLISHING (KDP)

KDP is a great first step to getting your book out into the world and into the hands of your prospects. There is really no faster, easier, and affordable way to go from words on the screen to books in your prospects' hands.

This is why I am appreciative of Amazon and thankful they keep making their process easier and easier for us.

What you need to know that I will expand on next in *"Distribution"* is that Amazon is in the sales and marketing business. They are not printers. While we could argue they allow you to *"publish"* your book, they are not in the business to help you maximize it to the fullest potential, all that you can. With that being said, I use them every single time I launch one of my own, for the Kindle version. This book is no different.

KDP does have some really great advantages in specific areas. Printing and pricing are just a few of them. You can get printed copies in your hands in record time. They look good, everyone's happy, and depending on page count, they can cost as little as $2.15 per paperback. Yes, you heard me correctly. I will give them that. KDP does kind of nail it on getting affordable copies, in most instances.

The caveat I share with all my audiences and author clients is that: *You may or may not want to use the physical printing side of this for your final production run.*

While Amazon does take the print order, they DO NOT fulfill it. They have partnered with independent printers across the country and maybe the world so that you have a fast turnaround time, as well as good quality. They, however, may not be exact or the best.

A fun little game to play is flip to the back of any book you suspect that may be from an Amazon printing partner—*or even if you know it is and you're simply curious to know where it's from.* On the last page you will see near the bottom the city, state, month, and year it was printed. I just grabbed a couple of my original book and books from other authors and combined; there were three recurring locations:

- **Columbia, SC**

- **Lexington, KY**

- **Middleton, DE**

Perhaps this is because I am located in Detroit, MI, and they are the closest to the east coast? While I've printed some of my first books with KDP in the past, and they turned out *"good,"* they are a noticeable difference from my newest ones, and especially this one which I believe looks **"GREAT!"** The inner workings of how they actually pull this off could be endless, and I'm sure it is a fascinating story. It would be an excellent documentary to watch on Prime...of course—*not Netflix.*

Whether that happens in the future, and they reveal it or not, you want to keep in mind that depending on how loaded your book—*may or may not be*—with charts, graphics, images, and basically anything other than text. Especially with color, it will affect the final printing. Depending on who you choose to print your final book with, these content editions may enhance or diminish your business book.

The goal is to always to hit it right the first time, and the likelihood that you will COMPLETELY change the cover is slim.

Another key area you always want to keep an eye on is binding. The design will literally get down to the millimeter, whatever the color is on the binding, and text that *"wraps"* from the front to the back of your book. In most instances, you'll be spot on or really close; there are the factors of the page count that will affect the design.

If you finalized your book front cover design BEFORE the final manuscript OR added to the manuscript after the cover design was complete, I would encourage you to check with your graphic designer the overall dimensions of the book again. *Even 5-10 pages, while not an enormous amount of paper, can alter it enough that it's not pixel-perfect.* Combine that with perhaps choosing a variety of printers (KDP) depending on where you live, and at the very least, you'll want more wiggle room.

The best thing you could do, however, is to simply start with BookBaby *(www.ExpertAuthorityEffect.com/BookBaby)*, who printed this gem and had real people going through a pre-press process in real life before it even went to print.

Even if the design and color are simple, you still have to deal with the spine's text. You're going to want a page count over 110-120 pages for the ability to have a spine with the book's name that's large and legible enough for your ideal reader to make sense of the text. You don't want to go crazy in trying to decide if 8.75pt font or 9.25pt is better. Both are too small.

I will say again, *"Don't make your business book too long.* I advise 120-180 page business books with a 190-200 page maximum. The longer your book is, the longer it will take to extract your expertise. You also have more to account for with the design, more pages, and your printing cost will jump up significantly starting in the 201 plus page arena—*in most cases.*

If your expertise demands it, it's not that expensive overall, especially since it's a business investment, go for it! However, keep in mind all these *"little things"* affect the *"big things."* I advise doing this when you have some time and leeway. However, I also designed my method for eight weeks because the likelihood of you ever really having *"downtime"* is slim. **The real travesty is that the longer the book is, the less likely your prospects will get through it. When they do, it will take longer, and they still have to implement your strategy or idea.**

If you have an opportunity to speak at a conference and get your books in the audience's hands versus NOT, pick one color and print, don't miss an opportunity because you spent weeks perfecting the binding that no one other than you and me will really notice. Also, never do a sub-par job. Clear as mud, right? Excellent!

I want to reiterate the most important reason:

"Your prospects won't finish it and implement your expertise, to realize their own transformation."

Once you feel it all looks good and you've filled in all the required boxes, it's time to *"Push the Button,"* and hit *"Submit!"* You'll be told it will be reviewed and could take up to 24 hours. You should receive some emails confirming the action you just took.

Once you get the next set of emails from KDP—*within 24 hours*, it will give you an option to get up to five *"Author Copies"* before you make the book available to the public. I always advise getting all five and looking them over, seeing how they feel, and making sure everything is printed the way you want.

Whether you choose KDP—or *BookBaby*—as your final printer, Print-On-Demand (POD) has many benefits, which is why we leverage this method.

You won't ever be stuck with 100,000 plus copies that didn't turn out the way you wanted. While the goal isn't to make unlimited changes, know that at any point in time, you can tweak your business book relatively easily. This is incredibly beneficial for updating and enhancing it for the following year's re-launch.

Once you're happy, simply go into KDP and make it fully published for the world to purchase!

BOOKBABY

Working with our premier partner, BookBaby, is one of the smartest things you can do for printing not only high-quality paperback versions of your book but also for the expanded distribution through their worldwide network.

While KDP is great for getting your book done and out there, when you're ready to knock it out of the park with a hardcover version with a case jacket and have it professionally done right the first time, I advise you use BookBaby. BookBaby is 100% Made in the USA, and they do all their printing stateside in New Jersey for the highest level of quality control for your business book.

As if this wasn't great enough, *all you have to do is order a minimum of 25 copies of your book with their distribution package, and they will connect to Amazon for all your Print-On-Demand (POD) needs moving forward, ensuring every copy of your book is the same experience and standard of excellence for your reader.*

Hardcover
BookBaby

This is also where our premier partner BookBaby comes in for hardcover printing. An incredible benefit of BookBaby is that they are the nation's leading self-publishing company. They specialize in Print-On-Demand (POD) and they also have the most robust connections through their partnership networks—*including Amazon.*

48 HOUR BOOKS

I also want to give a big shout-out to 48 Hour Books, who have the fastest turnaround times while maintaining the highest professional quality, and specialized prints available. This includes advanced options such as foil, and Diamond 3D Covers for short-run prints up to 500 copies—*per order.* I was thrilled with them, and so were my guests at my VIP in-person event that we did everything in a matter of weeks. I recommend them for specialized, limited edition, and event copies. Who knows, you may be holding one of the autographed limited editions right now.

The only downside of this is that they **DO NOT** offer Print-On-Demand (POD) integration with Amazon the same way BookBaby does.

They are another premier partner of ours, and we will continue to use them and advise you do too. (www.ExpertAuthorityEffect.com/48HourBooks)

OFFSET

In a nutshell, offset offers the best prices for both paperback and hardcover. Larger quantities are required—*1,000 plus minimum in most cases.* You will want the design 150% complete, approved, and tested before the full run print.

ISBN

The International Standard Book Number, or ISBN, is a unique 10-digit number assigned to every published book in the world.

An ISBN identifies a title's binding, edition, and publisher. An EAN, or European Article Number, is a 13-digit number assigned to every book to provide a unique identifier for international distributors.

The 10-digit ISBN is converted to a 13-digit EAN by adding a 978 prefix and changing the last digit.

To publish a book, you need an ISBN. We make ISBNs available to any business publishing their business book, at a savings through our IWDNow Publishing imprint, over Bowkers–*current*–$125 apiece price.

Through our Expert Authority Effect™ Publishing imprint ISBN's are included at no extra cost for our concierge-level authors, in addition to properly registering, setting them up, and applying them to their book on your behalf.

PRINT OPTIONS

Interior and Paper Type

Black and white interior with white paper

This is the simplest, easiest, and classic go-to that I not only advise but could very well be a great option for you. There is no confusion. It eliminates multiple refinements and gives you the highest contrast. If you want your book done and printed, this is a great option. Depending on your subject matter and length of the book, this may very well be one of your final steps. Click-click. Done.

Caveat - Conversely, also depending on your subject matter and length of the book, you may want to give your readers a break. While bright white looks good, it is also a higher strain on the eyes for prolonged periods of time. Know your audience, and think about what they would prefer most. I did my first few books with the black and white interior on white paper, my most recent books, however, especially the hardcovers, like this one, I have used:

Black and white interior with cream paper

This has been my recent favorite with the last three books compared to my first two for both paperback and hardcover. For **The Expert Authority Effect™**, I went with hardcover and a #70lb. cream paper that was still high contrast and easy to read, but also easy on the eyes. It gives a thicker, more luxurious feel in your hands. The cover was an elegant matte finish with a stunning case jacket and binding. Everyone loved the content, and they were beyond impressed with the print quality. It was the first book where I switched, and I'm glad I did. You're reading this now on cream paper, whether it's paperback or hardcover–*sorry Kindle*–for this exact reason, and I hope you're enjoying it.

This will be a personal decision for you and your business book. Depending on your subject matter, you might know right now from the start that you want cream paper, *fantastic! Go for it!* You may have only seen white and are now considering it. Ultimately think about your ideal reader and what they will enjoy most. Suppose you're pushing 150 to 180 plus pages. In that case, I'd advise using cream, especially for the hardcover, to increase the likelihood your ideal reader has a great reading experience while retaining and implementing more of your expertise.

If you have more of a workbook style for most of the content—*as I had early on in this book to get you started*, white will be fine. If your content, is more *"energetic"* versus *"relaxed,"* I would go white regardless of length. You want the tone of the paper to match the contents and the feel of the book. Consider also images and color. White will be best.

Use your best judgment, and don't take too long deciding either. Nobody can praise–*or complain*–about your business book if it's not in their hands. You can always tweak and adjust. However, don't make this an ongoing habit after you're already done.

Ice isn't the only one who can benefit from cream; you and your business book will also.

Color interior with white paper

Color is great for adding life to your charts, graphs, and images and will appear best on white paper. Depending on the graphic design, layout, and image choices, this could give your book the extra shine you and it deserve. You will pay a premium, but who cares! You're worth it, right?

Make sure it looks impressive in B&W—*the color will only amplify the truth.* Whether it's your business book, promotional banner, your logo, if it doesn't *"POP!"* in black and white, the color won't help; it will hurt it. Keep this in mind, but don't be shy about color either. If it makes sense for you, as it did with some of our authors and me, your prospects will love it.

Trim Size

6x9 | There are more than a dozen. Don't complicate it. I will remind you again to keep it simple and go with 6x9.

Bleed Settings | Bleed refers to how much of the ink will *"bleed"* off the page. Think of your favorite magazines, such as Entrepreneur, Forbes, Inc., or Robb Report, etc. The full-page images–*ads or otherwise*– would be considered *"Full Bleed"* since the image–*and ink, respectively*–

"Bleed" off the edge of the paper. The process they put them through is impressive as they must print all the way to the edge. For centuries, the only way to do this was on larger paper with the full image and then physically cut each page down to fit.

You more than likely won't need to do this; if however, you decide to, you will need to select:

- **Bleed** (PDF Only)

Thankfully, we don't need to waste–*and pay for*–extra paper and cutting it, as well as ink, and hope it all gets glued together correctly.

Simply select:

- **No Bleed**

and you'll be good to go.

Paperback Cover Finish

There are what may seem like endless possibilities for every aspect of the publishing process. Depending on who you choose to trust with the printing and distribution of your book, they may only increase depending on the printer's competency and experience. For the sake of illustration, I've kept everything focused on Amazon (KDP) for now, and they offer two:

Glossy

Very common, not bad, I've done it, you're welcome to, it's not bad. However, *my official position on what I advise is:*

Matte

It lasts longer. Glossy is generally a plastic coating. The more the books are banged around during shipping and handling, going to your event, people taking time to read it, folding it, creasing it, taking notes, edges can become *"worn"* and the seal can break. My first book, **"Video Marketing for Business Owners,"** was originally glossy. Again, not bad, but matte is better for this reason alone.

It looks classier. As much as you want to show off your newly written and published business book, you don't need to shrink-wrap the thing to get attention. ***You just wrote and published an entire business book!*** *That alone speaks volumes!* Let it.

My personal favorite. Photographs at book signings. No one talks about this, and I think that's a shame. Once I told some friends, colleagues, and other publishers, they followed suit.

You've made it this far, you did your best, and my goal with every one of our authors is to make the book such top-notch quality, as I've shared with you through each step of this entire book–*you won't need to touch it for at least one year*–until your next re-launch.

Keep focused on promoting, serving, and leveraging the asset you've just created.

It was my first book when I noticed the photo was not stellar. With a seventeen plus year professional career in front of and behind the camera for both photo and video, I tend to notice things most people miss. This was when I decided to switch to a matte finish. My prediction came true and has stayed true, and now I love sharing the secret with everyone, so they don't need to waste a minimum of a year and multiple shipments to narrow it down.

Choose matte the first time and focus on creating memories in the photos, with your book.

Distribution

PRINT

Books are online AND offline, is your book covered?
(intentional case jacket pun)

Of course, you're going to ask,

"*Can you get my book on Amazon??*"

Amazon

Of course, if you're talking to, or have talked to a publisher who can't get you on Amazon. This might be an indicator of their level of excellence and professionalism. Publishing is their business and they cannot help you get on the largest online retailer in the world, THAT STARTED WITH BOOKS, decades ago in 1994—*They may, just may, have some insights on it.* What does that tell you about the person you're talking to?

Additionally, they shouldn't be bad-mouthing Amazon either! Amazon is awesome, If you don't think so, you're doing it wrong. If you think,

"They're taking too much," then you're thinking, and playing too small.

Now you've done your homework and will probably ask about:

Barnes & Noble

Still, a *"YES"* and I advise you to go this route as well. Barnes & Noble is the largest retail bookseller in the United States, with over 650 bookstores throughout the country, plus 700 college bookstores. It's one of my favorite places to walk into, to this day.

What may not be on your radar is:

Books-A-Million

We already know who is number one, but did you know that Books-A-Million is the second largest book retailer in the nation? Currently, the company operates over 250 stores in 31 states—*and the District of Columbia*. Like most companies, they also sell online. *You should never limit yourself in business, and this is no exception.*

Powell's Books

Who is the largest independent new and used bookstore in the world? Meet Powell's Books; they are another avenue you should be distributed to. With all that opportunity, we haven't even scratched the surface yet!

Ingram

Ingram is also one of the world's largest distributors of books. If you'd like to get your book in practically any store, making it available for sale to more than 39,000 online retailers, Ingram is the way to go.

Baker & Taylor

Baker & Taylor distributes books to more than 36,000 libraries, institutions, and retailers in more than 120 countries. They're not a buzzword like *"Amazon."* Unless you've researched them, been, or are in the industry, you probably didn't know they existed. That doesn't mean they won't be a huge asset for your endeavor.

Don't skip them either.

There are even more, but I must get your book published, not write a dissertation on distribution.

KINDLE/EBOOKS

Our buddies Amazon and Barne's & Noble are back on the eBook list for obvious reasons, and joining them are their best friends:

Apple Books

Also, a *"YES!"* I advise you to publish and promote here as well. Apple is excellent at marketing and cornering markets, and for the same reason, **Expert Authority Effect™ Interviews** is on iTunes. It is the same reason you should have your book on Apple Books. It's crazy to be able to just say, *"It's Apple,"* and I don't need to write a paragraph or two, but you get it, and that is precisely what I'm going to do. Thanks Apple!

I'm smiling right now because you should remember I did the same for *"Disney"* in Positioning. The irony, and not a coincidence, is the history of Disney and Apple through Pixar. If you're unfamiliar, I encourage you to read and watch documentaries on it.

When you truly implement **The Expert Authority Effect™** in your business as they have, your partnerships will rise in caliber as well.

Imagine someone saying the same about your company:

"It's _____" and people just "Get it."

Scribd

Scribd is basically the *"Netflix for books."* They have a cloud-based catalog that includes stories, essays, academic papers, as well as books from nearly 1,000 publishers worldwide. They operate with a monthly subscription model that will make your book available to Scribd members. There are also industry leaders for Great Britain, Germany, Japan, as well as many others. A point should be made about book distribution:

"Amazon is the biggest name in town, but not the only. Distribute on them all."

Finish your book, and this part will be 100x more valuable than a grocery list of teaser opportunities that you can't even access until you're done.

AUDIOBOOKS

Audiobooks are a great way to get your message out to existing readers in a different and exciting format and reach new ones. Audiobooks have steadily risen over the last decade and continue to be a very popular and growing medium—*thanks to sites like Audible*—for books in general and business leaders who have limited time and are looking to maximize it.

You may be listening to me right now on the audiobook version, talking about audiobooks. Pretty surreal, huh? Welcome to my life publishing this book—*on business book publishing.*

If you would like to listen to the Audible version of **The Expert Authority Effect™ Publishing Method,** I invite you to do so at: *www.ExpertAuthorityEffect.com/EAPubAudible*

I encourage you to have your audiobook version professionally produced in studio as I have, once you have finished your book.

With all of these items complete, get yourself ready to promote this puppy!—*even though I know you already followed my directions and have already started the promotion process.*

"Publicity is absolutely critical. A good PR story is infinitely more effective than a front-page ad."

~ Richard Branson

Publicity

Y ay for recurring themes! You should know by now; whether it's day one or a month plus to launch, your new business book should NOT be a *"Best Kept Secret."*

This chapter really should be called *"Promoting It Some More,"* but that wouldn't fit the theme of clear, concise, one-word chapter titles. It also could be 50-100 chapters—*if that were the case*—because on the slim chance you haven't picked up on the recurring undertone yet:

YOU SHOULD BE PROMOTING YOUR BUSINESS BOOK LAUNCH EVERY DAY, NO MATTER WHERE YOU ARE IN THE PROCESS.

It's time for your **Expert Authority Effect™ Publishing Method** first Class VIP Book Launch Month!...countdown to launch day.

Day 1, Week 1

Make an announcement and promote.

We've established that, but what about the month leading up to launch day?

This is why there is an entire chapter dedicated to it.

While you can have your book written, edited, formatted, be sure to continue the promotion, and like the rest of my method, we are running it simultaneously.

This is normal and to be expected. As I mentioned earlier in the book, before we even started Chapter 2: PLAN, I wanted the book to be written chronologically to be as easy as possible to follow. The reality is you will need to be doing multiple steps simultaneously.

This is another one. However, it's straightforward to follow since I can give you explicit days and steps to take on those days to ensure a successful launch.

If you have skipped ahead on ANYTHING up until this point, I'm not surprised, you're a successful entrepreneur, and you want the results. I will also ask that you jump back and complete anything that's outstanding, such as the author sales page and email marketing integrations I will be referencing, otherwise it will make no sense as to why it's important and what you should be doing to best leverage it throughout the **Expert Authority Effect™ Launch Sequence.**

Let's start with your timeline and important days to track milestones.

MAJOR DAYS YOU SHOULD BE PROMOTING:

EVERY DAY

For calendar purpose, the simplest thing you can do is get in the habit of tracking it weekly.

This is one of the primary reasons I created my method to be executed over eight weeks.

This is not only for tracking purposes, but to ensure your success, profitability–*and to keep you accountable*–before it gets too dragged out, life happens, you get bored, interest wains or another *"Opportunity,"* comes your way, and before the momentum is lost. Regardless of the reason, the focus is still the end result, and we're approaching the finish line. Keep reading.

CALENDAR PLANNING PURPOSES

While I could write a whole book on the launch sequence alone, I will share with you the shortened version, so a) you don't need to read a dictionary and b) so you can visualize and implement it more easily. You need to have all the rest completed for the specifics to be fully beneficial to you. *If you've skipped anything so far, go back and do it.*

Not my first caveat in the book, why stop now? Straight up, this is not the *"end all, be all, set in stone, only way to do a launch"* sequence, far from it, and I want to make that 1000% clear, it's a guide so you can wrap your head around milestones and have a discernible calendar to follow, I will elaborate on the individual tactics after I establish the timeline. As I've said no less than a dozen times already:

PROMOTE YOUR BUSINESS BOOK FROM DAY 1 AND DON'T STOP

This is no exception just because below, I go from day fifty-six down to thirty. You may already have your manuscript not only written but edited, revised, edited some more, and even ready for print.

Many authors have come to us both pre, and post *"publish"* after seeing my method and wanting to fill the gaps from their first or second go-around.

Every entrepreneur has a different existing audience network. The size of these variables, along with your goals for the launch, will determine your actual final launch sequence.

Remember, more promotion is always better than less, and yes, I will share specifics, but I want to establish the timeline first. The activity and times can vary depending on your business, desire, and capabilities, but the timeline won't, so we'll start there.

Literally, as I write this, another entrepreneur with a large group called, based on the email–*that I debated sending, but followed my own advice*–and wants me to now speak: to his group, have me on his shows–*both radio and TV*–as well as a partner for this launch, and marketing help with his organization.

That's also not the only good that came from it, but if it were, I'd still be smiling at the opportunity to serve another new audience. It's probably a good thing I hit *"Send,"* as you should too. You never know what good is ready to happen for you from someone, and it just takes one person.

So now that we're still in agreement let's get your wheels spinning even faster for your own launch.

Mark your calendars for the following days:

56 Days | Aside from launch day itself, this is the second—*arguably the most important and fun day of this experience.* You've been hearing me say *"Day 1, Week 1"* maybe just once at this point. They are one and the same. This is *"Announcement Day!"*

30 Days | This is the line of demarcation. If you haven't been promoting, or even announced it, you need to do that, today, like now.

21 Days | Three weeks left until launch. You should be ramping up the promotion.

14 Days | Two weeks left until launch. Ramp up promotion even more. While you should be doing it every time it happens, this is a good *"checkpoint"* to leverage all the social proof feedback support from the previous two weeks—*If you haven't started already.*

7 Days | One week left until launch, or *"Launch Day!"* Now it's real; if you haven't already, you're going to feel it, there 's no stopping it, no turning back, it's no longer an idea, or *"something you're doing"* or simply another *"date on the calendar"* it's hours away! Depending on the time of day you look, it could be anywhere from 145 hours away to 168 hours away, but it's no longer a matter of weeks and days. It's hours, and minutes. If your excitement is that of the week between Christmas and the New Year, you're right on track. It should also be the absolute latest you upload for Kindle/KDP Print.

4 Days | Today is the Friday before launch day. Now that the 72 Hour window has passed, your book should be on Amazon, congrats! But don't announce it just yet. That's why we have launch day. You can, however, reach out to those in your launch team and have them start leaving reviews. This starts signaling Amazon that you're up to something exciting and will boost you come launch day to climb the charts faster.

3 Days | Today is the Saturday before launch day. Enjoy your weekend with family and friends; let them share in your excitement for your new book.

2 Days | Today is the Sunday before launch. Enjoy the day with family and friends. Take a breather.

1 Day | Today is the Monday before launch. Take another deep breath today–*you'll need it*–but get back to work promoting, enjoy the anticipation and excitement before the big day tomorrow, you did it! Tomorrow it all comes to fruition. Tomorrow is a whole new level if you think it feels good to have it completed and on Amazon, document it, take photos, videos and celebrate, enjoy it, celebrate every minute of it because it will go by in the blink of an eye.

If you haven't done so yet, grab yourself your copy—*you gotta sell yourself first, right?* This will keep Amazon's ranking system activated and going. You can also invite your launch team and those closest to you to help prime the pump. *This isn't the launch day quite yet, but you want to start getting some sales, so Amazon takes notice, and you can see your categories as soon as possible on launch day.*

Amazon's clock is on the west coast of the United States. Pacific Time (PST), so 3 a.m. EST–*convert for your time zone*–is really the 24-hour start time period you want to aim for.

Oh, look, another caveat, you'll notice I said "*7 a.m.*" earlier, and perhaps you saw the launch of this book real-time and noticed it said 7 a.m. also, why you ask? Great question:

"Most people are sleeping through the night."

I mean, it's not any more complicated than that. You have to decide what time is best for you and your audience. I recommend 7 a.m. since it's a nice balance between "*early enough to maximize the 24-hour window,*" and "*not so early your readers are not coherent yet.*"

The reality is if you've been promoting enough up to here, you'll wake up and have some Amazon sales. It's fun, looking forward to it again with this one. For my international audience, that helped make it possible throughout the time zones. Thank you.

You will most likely also see early afternoon–*lunchtime*–and early evening–*dinner time*–sales bumps which are a lot of fun because all they do is help you continue to move up the charts, and most importantly, impact your ideal reader who just invested in your book, as well as their time to read it.

Amazon tracks their sales on an hourly basis, so if you're speaking at a live event and can make an offer to the entire room to buy at once, by all means, go for it. This is one of the best ways, in addition to what tactics we're talking about, to ensure the highest number of sales and increase your chances with the Amazon Best Seller Ranking.

You do not, however, NEED TO do this, as the only way to start ranking and moving up the charts. This is why we focus the sales in the shortest period of time we can get within the 24-hour window–*to allow and account for*–international sales, factor in real-life scenarios, and your prospects and clients' daily lives. The reality is the bulk of all your sales will happen from 7 a.m. EST to 7 p.m. EST with some before and after adding to and further supporting the ranking and maintaining it.

You may be wondering what are the:

Fun & Easy Ways to Generate Publicity and Promote Your Launch

- **Book Sales Page**
- **Launch Team**
- **Email Broadcast Campaign**
- **Social Media Posts**
- **LinkedIn Event**
- **Facebook Event**
- **Livestream**
- **Live Event Speaking**
- **Podcast Interview Tour**
- **Press Releases**
- **Radio & TV**
- **VIP Book Launch LIVE! In-Person Event**

These are in no particular order, but I did think about the *"lowest hanging fruit"* as with the **Expert Authority Effect™ Evidence Intelligence Gathering Process,** with what you can do NOW, without approval, or someone else's timeline being a factor vs. what is still easy. Still, you may be on someone else's calendar.

The more you can fit into your launch sequence timeline, the better, but don't turn anything down–*really for any reason*–let alone because *"it's a few days or weeks past launch."*

Remember what I said earlier? ***"More Promo > Less"***

Book Sales Page

Amazon does not give you access to the information from your buyers. You're sending them traffic, and they're keeping it all. You don't know who anyone is, and there is no way to say *"THANK YOU!"* I have a problem with this and a problem with not being able to follow up down the road, stay in touch, and add even more value as time goes on. When someone says *"Congrats!"* and invest their hard-earned money with you, the relationship between the two of you has changed. You always want to be able to offer them a way to receive more value from you. At the least, a name and email is a great place to start, but it won't happen without a book sales page.

Launch Team

The more, the merrier, am I right!? It's not a party if it's only you. No one ever said you have to launch the book on your own. Build synergy, have fun. This is your moment so prepare to shine. Think of those that: a) already support you b) have supported you in the past. The more recent, the better, but in a sentence or less; *"If you do business with them, they can do business with you."*

Email Broadcast Campaign

Realistically, *"book"* or not, you should always be building your list. This should be self-explanatory, but email is a great way to keep everyone on the same cadence in the weeks leading up to launch—*and after.* If all someone on your launch team is willing to do is one email, GREAT! Have them send it on LAUNCH DAY! letting their audience know your book is available. I advise you **DO NOT** skip this method.

Social Media Posts. I wouldn't say they're in the same caliber as *"Disney"* or *"Apple."* Still, I highly suspect you, as well as the social media manager on your team, *"Get it,"* I do, however, feel compelled to say more, so: *"Use social media to your advantage, share specific posts about your book and launch."* Okay, now we're both happy.

LinkedIn Outreach & Event Since we're talking business, LinkedIn is a hotbed for business professionals. Leverage your LinkedIn network for outreach and an event for launch day.

Facebook Outreach & Event
Facebook may not be geared for business professionals; however, many people forget that business professionals are also real live people with families, friends, and lives. Leverage your Facebook network for outreach and an event for launch day. Just realize it's not LinkedIn.

Livestream Personally, video and livestreaming are my favorite ways to share messages. Most people love videos. They're engaging, effective, fun, and profitable, which are some of the reasons I wrote my first book, **Video Marketing For Business Owners,** in 2012. Nearly all the platforms offer this option now, do it, and the more others can host you on theirs, even better. You should 1000% host a livestream for your launch.

Live Event Speaking Live event speaking to large audiences is still–*arguably*–the #1 way to get your message out, add value, influence a room, and do a month to a quarter's worth of work in an hour.

They are also my absolute favorite! This is really where I started, even before business, and I'm sure you did as well, and if not, it now can be part of your repertoire.

If you'd like me to speak to your group on Business Book Publishing, just ask; I'd be happy to. Simply go to:

www.ExpertAuthorityEffect.com/BookMario or call (313) 288-2275.

Podcast Interview Tour I can tell you that lining up your podcast interviews is a great way to promote your book, both prior to and post-launch. You may also enroll the podcast host in your launch team. Long before I even launched **Expert Authority Effect™ Interviews,** I was doing radio, podcast, and TV interviews. I highly recommend it, I love sharing when I'm a guest, and as a host, I've had the pleasure of connecting with hundreds of great authors and entrepreneurs like you. Do both.

PRESS RELEASES (*RELEASEWIRE & PRNEWSWIRE*)

Press releases are nothing new; I'm sure you've either already done them or read some. Using them for your book launch is something I advise that most overlook. There's something about a good press release that will make it really permanent for years to come. You can choose how many make sense for you before launch, but doing a press release post-launch, with the results, testimonials of early and first readers should be on your to-do list.

Radio & TV

Another avenue you've most likely already leveraged as I have, and if it makes sense for you, I advise it. However, in most cases, you will be on someone else's calendar, do it anyhow if you are capable and able to this launch cycle.

VIP Book Launch LIVE! In-Person Event

First-class is your thing, and this is the way to do it. When doing your best just isn't good enough, hosting an epic VIP Book Launch LIVE! Event will be the cherry on top and a night to remember. I will never forget the one I threw for **The Expert Authority Effect™**. Twenty-eight floors up, renting out the main room with live music, open bar, 5-star chef-prepared food, award-winning author clients, closest friends in business, and my family. Little did I know it would be the last time I would be able to take dad to one of my favorite places to spoil him and mom and this time with their brothers and sisters.

I've helped my author clients with their events also, and every time, fun is had, books are signed, laughter is heard, tears are shed, memories are made, and magic happens. I HIGHLY, HIGHLY, HIGHLY advise this as soon as it's right for you. Also, do it right. Don't invite people just to invite them. Make it count and close the doors.

These are simply a few ideas that work very well that I've incorporated in my own personal launches as well as all of my author client launches. As long as you follow my game plan and have the core publicity rock solid, I have really never said *"No"* to additional ideas that support your launch on an individual basis. Anything you've seen another author do, you know your ideal reader prospects would find value in it, do it.

With all that being said, it's nowhere's near what's out there. I do, however, hope it has been a great primer for you, and your wheels are at an all-time high spin now.

Regardless of the medium:

"Promote Your Book Daily, and Don't Stop, Even After Launch."

With all these assets in your launch arsenal, you are ready for your day to remember!

LAUNCH DAY!

7 a.m. EST Tuesday, a.k.a. Launch Day!

No matter what, enjoy yourself and celebrate. You did it! You not only WROTE your book, but you also PUBLISHED IT. Today you get to release it into the world and perhaps even have the best-selling day you've ever had.

You have sold some copies already, and ideally, you're already getting feedback on how great your business book is, but don't let that stop you.

PUSH, it's one day. *You haven't gotten this far, only to get this far.* No matter what happens with Amazon's webpage, keep pushing, and keep selling.

If you're aiming to reach the coveted *"Bestseller"* status, **keep pushing even if you think the website says it.** You don't want to simply *"hit it."* You want to *"blow by it,"* remember, it's not just some numbers on a screen. These are real people, with real lives and families you're impacting. By all means, go for it, but keep your priorities and goal straight. Be aware I've also seen where Amazon pretty much froze rankings for 4-5 days— *all of which still counts as long as you have the best sales; it's just that the site doesn't reflect it in a timely fashion.*

The last thing I'll add here is: *"Regardless of the status you rank for, on Amazon, it doesn't take away from anything you've done and already achieved and will continue to do."*

I've seen some really great people–*outside of my method*–absolutely have their identity decimated, and even stopped in business because they were promised something that never happened, OR it DID HAPPEN, and they didn't have the book finished on time–*gaming the system with "pre-sale" orders*–but not being able to deliver on their expertise.

I SINCERELY HOPE you blow by all these rankings and become #1 not only in your categories but in all of Amazon. People do it every day.

I'm also saying, regardless of where you end up, it's not a make or break anything if your goal is to serve your audience at a higher level truly, and you're looking for more than just another vanity metric.

Furthermore, there are those people who may not give much credence to *"Amazon"* bestselling—*even if you attain it*, as well as *"Wall Street Journal Best Selling,"* and for the few who make *"New York Times Best Selling,"* they say, *"They just bought the title,"*—*and some do.*

To these uplifting, inspiring, optimistic individuals, I say: *"Finish your 1st book, then open your mouth."* Statues are never erected of critics.

I personally really enjoyed achieving #1 Best Selling Author because it didn't happen the 1st time–*even though I had 3-5x more sales than most do, who get it.* Remember the nuthouse of all those categories from earlier? They were the straw that broke the camel's back. It wasn't until five years later, on a re-launch, that this was rectified. The upside was I never stopped serving, my audience grew, and I not only cleared #1 that day but also *"International."* **The categories are a make-or-break thing, don't get them wrong.**

I especially liked getting it not just once, but the second time as well, which brought in *"2x INTERNATIONAL Best-Selling Author."* Don't forget to update all your branding with your new positioning, along with your book cover, especially when you have more than one.

You may be thinking, *"Why not 3x, 4x, 5x?."* It's not a big deal; I have the books and know I could achieve it—*along with Wall Street Journal and USA Today.* Let me ask you, how do you like the book so far? Would it make the content any stronger or weaker? As I've mentioned, I know many personally, including New York Times Best Sellers, and while everything *"helped,"* no one has said: *"The status alone was the magic."*

Between you and me, a good portion have come to me asking what I'm doing looking for insight on marketing for their re-launch campaign. The world is different now than five years ago, let alone ten or twenty.

There will be a point that I will consider doing a launch that is ten to one hundred times larger than the second edition of this was, but I can say now it won't be for the status. It will be to reach you.

As I personally near the end of my book, I'm beyond excited for how tight the content is; I have no doubt you are running with it, enjoying it, and I'm so glad it's now in your hands.

Going back to what I enjoyed most from **The Expert Authority Effect™ Launch,** was I decided to *"Not get hung up"* on the ranking. I actually surprised our authors to a private dinner the night before the event, we had a blast, and I remember making that memory, the smiles on their faces, and hearing them share what their book did for them, of which I had a hand in making happen, as I do again now with you.

I have never, and will never take it lightly or for granted. As I tear up now writing this last bit thinking about walking them out, and as we all went into the parking lot, I opened the door of my Cadillac, sat down—*yes, I checked*—and started crying, because it happened again!

What was surreal was they did too, and then they all came back over to congratulate me. You're welcome to sit near the computer for 48 hours straight, anxiously texting, messaging, and really begging people to grab a copy for a whopping 99 cents; I, however, don't advise it.

This is my method, and you don't need to. Focus on the real goal and end game, not the short term. If that's what you wanted and are still reading, awesome, I hope it helped you change your tune. Since I know that's not you, that's why these other 100 pages of detail exist.

While I know I've gone into more detail explaining, in as much detail as I feel you can reasonably digest without feedback between your weekly milestones, and is appropriate for a book, the reality is this has nothing to do with the book, and everything to do with your mindset and heart—*but sure, there's a cover and some words.* With that being said, the fact you have a book now, or another one and it was properly promoted this time, are the game-changers.

Realize this is a minimum of a 1M asset to your business, harnessed properly. This is what may very well be your first break in a few days—*or eight weeks*—even with your team, or a team behind you, if you're anything like me, it's going to be on your mind, in one of the *"Top 10"* spots, to ensure it's success. That is an excellent thing if you ask me.

Today, however, is when you smile, have fun, celebrate, and thank everyone graciously congratulating you. It's also a great day to do a livestream—*even if you don't love them*—because there's no way you won't be on cloud nine, and you won't be able to hide it. *Capture this moment.*

Not only is it fun to go back to in the future, share with others, but *it also makes killer marketing snippets for your next launches* <<< read *that again.*

There could be some people who have been *"meaning to"* get a copy of your book but have been *"too busy,"* if they haven't in the last few days, today would be a good day to have someone do a final follow up for increased sales and get the great material in their hands.

Some are just last minute by nature; others legit have been speaking and traveling, doing their own launches, and have had a packed schedule. No judgment either way; if they said they wanted a copy or one hundred plus copies, and you know it will help them, it would be a disservice for them not to have it; I mean, didn't we say we're doing this to help more people?

You're in the zone; they shared interest, stay in the zone, serve them.

There are also in-person parties as an option you've heard me mention; I highly recommend this as well. You know, I was going to go into more detail and be like, *"Let me tell you about your special launch day and all it's possibilities,"* but I'm smiling ear to ear, imagining you, slight tear in my eye, and just decided:

YOU TELL ME, ABOUT YOURS!

"Just because you're writing it, doesn't mean you can't be selling it."

~ Mario Fachini

INCREASE YOUR AUTHORITY, CREDIBILITY, & PROFILE

We talked about this a little earlier. The root word of *"Authority"* is *"Author."* Publishing your business book shows commitment, and commitment is one way your credibility is transformed into increased trust and profit.

Your prospects will see you didn't just talk about it; you did it.

You put the utmost care and attention into your business and treat it as such, and they know if you can do it on your own, they can trust you with theirs. You are not just another–*Insert Your Business Niche Here* –in the world, only out to get the sale. You show care.

The most important thing for every business is the character and integrity of the owner, which is the type of person you must be, not just hope to be. It can't be faked. When you get this right, you won't have a reputation problem. However, every business, both on and offline, has a reputation and perception of how it's known in the eyes of the clients and prospects.

Your business book will raise your profile in the eyes of your prospects and clients.

NEW OPPORTUNITIES WILL FIND YOU

There are venues, communities, and opportunities that are reserved for authors, unless you are an author, you don't get in. These become unlocked for you, and the possibilities are endless. I've met some of the most exceptional people on earth behind these closed doors.

- **Acquire New High Net-Worth Clients**
- **Adding Value & Creating a Lasting Impact**
- **Legacy**

As if everything else wasn't enough, this could arguably be the best way to profit from your business book.

RELATIONSHIPS

This is up there, perhaps tied with legacy. The quality of relationships you attract into your life rises, both personally and professionally. You will profit significantly in all senses of the word; overall, your life as a whole will be better off for it.

Here is another primer list of some specific tactical examples of how your business book will help you achieve your desired outcomes listed above.

- **Direct Book Sales**
- **Book Signings**
- **Events**
- **Paid Speaking**
- **Consulting**
- **1:1 Client Coaching**
- **Group Coaching**
- **Masterminds**
- **Podcast Interviews**
- **Services**
- **Digital Products**
- **Physical Products**
- **Training**
- **Taxes**

Some of these will be obvious, some may be new to you, and reading over the list again, I'm confident you're already doing half of them to the vast majority, if not all of them already—*or have.* In the vein of full transparency, I'm not going to break these down over the next twenty to thirty pages, or even five to ten, and here's why: a) We've already covered a lot of them in detail b) I'm already approaching 42,000 words and every word I type like this one makes me feel like I'm at the pump c) the other night I wigged out when I tested this manuscript size from 8.5x11 to 6x9 before sending to my formatting team—*the page count was at 308* d) you already have a successful business, and like I just mentioned this is nothing new, your business book will amplify everything and even more than what's here, and you know it—*thanks for your understanding.*

Last but not least, E) Which is what we will both get if we don't stay in our **Expert Authority Effect™ Genius Zone,** leveraging our expertise for actually serving our prospects and clients—*avoiding falling down the rabbit hole, and additionally the recurring theme through the entire book, I need to get this in your hands and not spend weeks, let alone months "perfecting it."*

I'll know over the next year if you loved it or hated it, that's the beauty, you can say whatever you want, it's your book. There are endless ways to profit from it, but nothing happens until it's out of YOUR hands and into everyone else's.

This is just the beginning; get it done. None of these ways matter unless you do. Even worse, you won't be able to move into something that is arguably even more important:

"So, whatever you wish that others would do to you, do also to them, for this is the Law and the Prophets."

~ Jesus

Philanthropy

THE GOLDEN RULE

Your book itself is a way to give back and share your expertise and wisdom with the world—*as well you should.*

It is also a new conduit, and business model, that you can use for personal and professional gain. I, however, encourage you to see the world as full of abundant opportunities.

This is not the end, merely the beginning. It's time to continue thinking beyond the book, as this is also virtually limitless.

Here is another primer list to keep those wheels spinning faster than ever.

- **Gifting the Audience Incentive**

The beauty is this strategy works both virtually as well as in person.

Personally, I've used my books as incentives virtually, especially livestreams, webinars, guest interviews, etc. It originated, however, from my initial in-person speeches. Whether you're the guest speaker or not, I can't think of one time; I was at an event where I offered to give away copies of any of my books, and they said *"no."* Additionally, nearly everyone wanted my book over the other *"Free Call,"* or *"$100 off your next purchase of $1,000 or more,"* the ones who didn't win asked to purchase copies, and regardless of which books I offered, they asked about getting copies of my others.

Not to mention, when I wasn't the guest speaker and had no intention of speaking, I was asked if I would *"Mind sharing about the book, for a few minutes."* If you could see my face right now, there is a smirk on it—*and yes of course, I got on the mic.* Even as seasoned as I am with events and networking, 2-5 minutes is still far faster to collect nearly the entire rooms business card than trying to *"network"* with every last person in a few short hours—*simply because they wanted to win my book, because I had one.*

This was also all within the first fifteen minutes of the one event, so afterward I thought to myself, *"wow, now what?"* I proceeded to simply enjoy myself and share more insights with those who asked, zero pressure, and less than ten minutes of effort—*if you don't count the years that went into the knowledge, and the few months to publish and launch it.*

Very little can match, let alone top, the perceived value, tangibility, and immediacy as a physical book can, especially in these environments.

- **Charity Partnership**

Different organization and purpose, but all the same advantages and ease of implementation. Charities love being attached to published authors and the simplicity of receiving the books and giving them to their winners, donors, or both.

- **Fundraiser Partnership**

I'm smirking, trying to think of something new to say, but it's the same *"rinse and repeat"* the difference is the group, what and who is getting it, but as far as you're concerned, it's just more books, you did the hard work already. Isn't this nice? This is another form of profit for you, time. This is now such a low-impact activity on your part. Why wouldn't you be leveraging it outside of business and helping more with your message?

- **Donation Giveaways**

Another avenue, same process. I'm sure you ***"get it"*** by now. I'll add this, make a list of all the companies, networks, organizations you already have ties to, ask your network, and continually add to it over the next year, prior to your re-launch.

- **Event's and Everything Else**

Literally, keep your books with you, you never know when you'll be at an event, and an opportunity will arise. Also, keep some sharpies in the book box as well so you can sign them on the spot. No one has told me they didn't want an autographed copy; they just wanted the book.

*Fun side note, I forgot my license at a store one time–I think computer parts–*and they had to prove the account was mine; you better believe I grabbed a copy from my trunk and came back, got done what I needed, autographed it, and gave it to the clerk. We both smiled and had a good day. While this was fun and memorable—*it hasn't worked at the airport for boarding a plane for me yet.* *Remaining Optimistic*

THE PIZZA HUT BOOK IT! PROGRAM

I remember them from when I was a kid, reading eighth grade-level books in third. I'm thrilled they were around for me and still are—*I just checked. www.ExpertAuthorityEffect.com/BookIt*

If you know someone or have an in, I'd love to partner with this great organization. Feel free to call: (313) 288-2275 or *www.ExpertAuthorityEffect.com/Contact*

SCHOLASTIC BOOK CLUB

Another great organization that has me smiling writing this, because as I grabbed the URL at the Scholastic website, *www.ExpertAuthorityEffect.com/ScholasticBookClub*, all thy memories of getting their flyer—*printed on what seemed like Kleenex,* came rushing back. Picking my selection and marking down the books I wanted with pencil on the soy-ink printed tissue that I could barely read. Being jealous on occasion of the other kids who also picked out the toy packages and other things. Ultimately none of that mattered because:

MY BOOKS WERE HERE!

Hearing the delivery person knock on the classroom door with a box full of books, the teacher stopping class, handing us our goodies, and knowing in a few short minutes I'd have what I had been anticipating for 7-10 days was so exciting! Such a great memory. Do you share a similar one?

Reliving this experience makes me a little teary-eyed because I'm seeing it so vividly right now sharing with you. I am being brought back to the third grade, realizing that's when I really started diving into books and not just casually reading, but consuming them. Every chance I got; I would ask if we could buy another one. I said *"we"* instead of *"I"* because I hadn't started my business yet—*I'm only about 7-8 here, not 12*, I didn't have my full-time weekly income yet, these were not just kids' books—*rarely kids' books*, I even got in trouble in grade school because I wasn't listening during library time; I was too bored. The books they had us check out–*ahhh, card catalogs, remember those*–were too easy for me, and often I would finish the book before we left for the day.

My mom and dad started buying eighth grade reading-level novels for me. I still wanted more books every week while taking longer than 30-45 minutes in class to get through.

I would bring them to school to read, but then got in trouble because one of the books was Peter Benchley's *"Beast."* I'll have to ask mom about her side of the story before this is published. What I'd really like is a recording of that call:

Teacher trying to get me in trouble—*again: "Mrs. Fachini, I wanted to let you know your son is reading some graphic material designed for someone five grades ahead of him."*

Mom: *"I know, I'm the one who bought it for him!"*

I'll fact-check that when I call her, but the books are still on the shelf in my old bedroom at the Fachini home.

I say all that to say this:

"You never know who, when, or where your book will change a life."

~ *Mario Fachini*

Conclusion

You also don't know when your book might just save a life. This is more than a simple primer, but again, *"the possibilities are endless"—I swear if that gets fact-checked or flagged for plagiarism—*some final joking aside:

You're here for a reason. God gave you the seeds of greatness, they are already inside of you, and now it's all getting released, not just from you to your book, but your book to the world.

I can't wait to hear YOUR success story!

In the spirit of philanthropy, I have:

A Gift For You

With a goal of keeping this book less than 200 pages—*so people don't think you're reading the yellow pages,* I've created *www.FREEBusinessBookPublishingCourse.com* for you as a complimentary companion to this book, where we can expand on the value already delivered. While I've been making fun of specifics in parts this entire time, the reality is that they are always relevant, and some of them don't translate well to print—*as you undoubtedly noticed in the nutso categories section.*

I invite you to join me inside:

www.FreeBusinessBookPublishingCourse.com

Where you will get your complimentary:

- Title generator *(Downloadable PDF)*
- Sub-Title Generator *(Downloadable PDF)*
- Expert Authority Effect™ Process Creation *(Downloadable PDF)*
- Promote, Promote, Promote!
- Expert Authority Effect™ Evidence Intelligence Gathering™ Guide
- Sharpen Your Writing!
- Book Structure Expanded Edition

- Category Research Video
- The expanded Expert Authority Effect™ Launch Sequence
- FAQs
- EAQs

Other additional deep dives and exclusive content!

Lastly, the content inside:
www.FREEBusinessBookPublishingCourse.com is updated on a fairly regular basis, so jump in and keep checking back.

It is my sincerest prayer that you enjoy—*and implement,* my gift to you as an additional way to pay it forward. That way, your message, business, and your life will always live on.

Epilogue

THANK YOU!

For investing your time with me, it's been my honor to share it with you. This is my life's passion on paper, and by far was the most emotional and mentally challenging one for me to write. My goal was to pull out all the stops, and to that end, I can now confidently say: *"I've done better than my best for you."* I hope you have enjoyed reading this as much as I've enjoyed writing it. I am very much looking forward to hearing the success story of **YOUR BOOK LAUNCH!**

As always, have a great day, and God Bless :)

Mario Fachini

About the Author

As a high school educated college dropout, Mario spent years as a dead-broke web designer wasting too much time chasing down—*the wrong*—clients, believing in his heart that the sky's the limit, but waking up every day feeling like the limits the sky.

Until he refined the publishing and enhanced the promotion from his first books to attract prospects to him, leveraging his expertise at his everyday disposal!

Now, he's one of the most in-demand business book marketing-centric publishers in the country, having author prospects now APPLY for his companies concierge services, thanking him for the opportunity, and sharing in the joy of their 55-day transformation, having helped his clients in total generate over $1 million in new sales.

Other Books by Mario

Video Marketing For Business Owners: *The Ultimate 7 Step Guide to Become the Expert, Authority, and Celebrity in Your Niche*

The IWDNow Freedom Platform™: *The World's #1 System to Build WordPress Websites Automatically!*

The Expert Authority Effect™: *Your 7-Step Brain Dead Simple Blueprint To Attract Your Ideal Dream Clients By Increasing Your Authority Positioning Today!*

My Rich Dad: *The 1 and Only 1-Step Success Formula to Unlimited Wealth*

Thank You

Thank You For Reading My Book!

I am always working on making my books the best they can be, and one of the ways I achieve this is through feedback.

I want to ask if you could leave me an honest review on Amazon and Audible–depending on how you "read" the book–so I can learn what you loved most about the book.

This also helps make a more significant impact and supports more businesses because we all know that items online with great reviews get picked first.

I would really love nothing more than to learn you didn't know me from Adam, read some reviews, maybe previewed the book, and decided to invest, loved it, and you ended up with your own book for your business. I would still, of course, ask you to leave a review, so I have that as feedback, but as I mentioned in the book, I am 100% looking to create the same synergistic effect I want for your business.

So, what do you say? Can you do that for me and help advance the mission before you go?

~ *Mario*

MORE PRAISE FOR

THE EXPERT AUTHORITY EFFECT™ PUBLISHING METHOD

"Hi, I'm Maryalice Coleman, I am an inner life coach, a mentor, author, and workshop leader, and I love helping women in a specific area.

I had hired people to help me with my book launch, I had hired people to help me with my website, and through that, NOTHING GOT DONE, and I wasted thousands of dollars. It was so frustrating for me, and I knew I needed to launch my book and I needed help with that. Well, Mario came into my radar, and I thought I'd reach out to him. And I am so glad that I did that! I can't even tell you.

The results were amazing for me, and such a wonderful relationship; he's great, he's just a great guy, He helps keep me focused on my work. But what he got done for me in three days, regarding my book launch. Unimaginable, you can't even imagine, nobody else could do it, nobody else even tried to do it. One person I hired was still spinning wheels at three months.

Mario is Santa Clause; I say that he is Santa Clause because there is a surprise every morning in my email working with him, with things I didn't even ask for but things he thought of ahead of time, to create beautiful graphics, to help me understand the process of the launch. To help me gain knowledge with even Facebook on how to do Facebook Ads, and there is so much more I learned from Mario.

So, if you need somebody to help you in your work, in whatever it might be, your website, or launching something, or creating, Mario is the guy to go to, And I can't say it enough, so, I would just, I don't know, I don't know what else to say because I am excited about working with Mario."

- Maryalice Coleman | CEO of Women's Growth Network

"Hi, I'm Barbara McLean, CEO of Karmic Media Group; I help non-profit executives to become more impactful leaders, to attract and engage donors, volunteers, and media. I've known Mario Fachini going on two and a half years now, and we've been working together for over a year and a half, and he has helped me to feel more confident in what I'm doing, to re-frame some of the thoughts that go through my head. You know those crazy thoughts when you're a solo entrepreneur, and you're working alone by yourself, you get some crazy thoughts, and he really helps me to re-frame those thoughts and to help me feel stronger and more confident with what I'm doing. He has also helped me a lot with approaching clients, potential clients, getting leads, lead generation, talking with them, to talk about what I do to frame it so that the pitch is comfortable for me because that was something I was very uncomfortable for me previously, the whole sales side of things, and actually now, I love doing sales now because it's "Just a conversation with customers" so that's been really fun to get over that and overcome and increase my skill set. He has also helped with some tactical things as well as strategic things. So, this is someone I highly recommend, and that it's enjoyable working with him, and I continue to work with him."

- **Barbara McLean** | CEO of Karmic Media Group

"Hi Michelle Duplechan, here from Duplechan Marketing Solutions, and I just wanted to say a few words about Mario's coaching program. Before I started his coaching program, I'd been in business for a few months, and I really wasn't the progress that I thought I could be; I didn't have a clear path, I was feeling overwhelmed, and I felt like I needed some guidance. Once I started working with Mario, he helped me to see that a lot of what I was going through had to do more with mindset than anything, he helped me to focus on what was important to focus on one or two things at a time and he inspired and encouraged me to break through those mental barriers that I was struggling with at the time. Since working with him, I've gotten my first couple of paying clients that I'm thrilled to be working with, and I'm well on my way to a growing thriving business. So, if you're struggling to get to the next level in your business or you just need some inspiration or encouragement or some guidance, give Mario a call; I know you will be glad you did."

- Michelle Duplechan | CEO of Duplechan Marketing Solutions

"It's been a pleasure working with IWDNow Marketing with Mario on the shooting and the advertising and the marketing for my practice. Initially, I was a little bit nervous, and when Mario came in, I wasn't sure if he was knowledgeable enough in the field of dentistry to be able to promote certain things and asked me questions, but there are certain things and whatnot, and I was really shocked about how prepared he was and how much he knew about the industry itself before he came in. So, he was very prepared, and that took the edge off for me and set me at ease to be able to do the marketing that I need for my practice. I really appreciated that, and I will; I would highly recommend him for anybody that needs any kind of marketing needs for their business."

- Dr. Sam Kamouni | Founder & CEO of Campus Dental

"Hi, my name is Rebecca Love; I'm the President of SONSIEL. I worked with Mario on an incredible video live stream for Facebook that was going out in front of the audience that generally wasn't familiar with Facebook Live Stream the level of precision, information, and experience that he brought to the table and made the experience seamless, timeless and also incredibly credible in the world that we're dealing with the virtual media today so I strongly recommend Mario for any future projects that you would have both for your business or personal. The future is really going to be going online, and you're going to need the best behind you to make sure that you appear the best you can. Thank you."

- Rebecca Love | President & Co-Founder of SONSIEL

"Hey everybody, I'm Nikki, with Nikki Incandela Photography, and I just met Mario this weekend. He's an amazing guy, super helpful, brilliant & intelligent, warm and fuzzy, approachable, and easy to talk to, so definitely check him out. Check out his photo, he gave me his business card, and seriously, he looks like big baller, I told him he doesn't look like he owns a casino, but he may own Vegas; great guy, check him out, thanks, Mario, for your help."

~ **Nikki Incandela** | Founder & CEO of Nikki Incandela Photography

"It's been very helpful. In fact, you helped me get it to number one on Amazon. So, thanks for that. I think I've thanked you a hundred times already. But now there's a hundred and one. But it's been helpful because people find it an interesting guide. It's a good way to get their information, their contact information and follow up with them. But it's also, more importantly, the guide for them to help them with color, style, the appropriate product, we call it application, applying the right product to the right situation. So, it's really helpful for them with that it gives them. It answers questions that they probably hadn't thought about asking before. And so, it positions us as the authority. So that's helpful for us.

But in addition to that, it also encourages them to want to go to our website and look at our frequently asked question videos, as well as our should ask question videos. And again, it answers them there, in multimedia, because sometimes people need to read something, sometimes they need to see it and hear it. Everybody learns in different ways. Personally, I learn through video, and in a little bit, my second modality would be audio, but you know, some of these folks that want to watch the video and see what I'm demonstrating on videos, they can do that. And again, it's very helpful for them. It creates bonding, which is nice because you have that rapport. And then by the time we get out there, in most cases, people are just asking, listen, we already know we're gonna do business with you. We did what you said, we Googled all the company names that we're considering with the right keyword and the word reviews at the very end, we looked at their reviews, we looked at your reviews, and you're clearly the company we're gonna go with. So that said, what's it going to cost? And that's before we even measure or take out samples.

So, you know, it kind of does, it does the selling for you, it's your people are presold, presifted, presorted, preselected and predisposed to do business with you if you do it that way. So, and, you know, thankfully, you were able to help get that book to the up on the, you know, number one on Amazon within the charts like that, because that is also added authority and credibility. So, what we've done with the content and what we've done with reviews is one thing, but without having the authority to be, you know, it'd be, it'd be more diluted it wouldn't have been as potent as it was. So, thank you for that."

~ Don Lovato | Founder & CEO of Carpet Source USA

"Pro Smiler and Host of "Expert Authority Effect™ Interviews," Thank You for creating the best podcast experience, and most importantly, thank you for walking me through the process of writing and publishing this book. Without your professional experience and guidance, this book would not have been possible in less than eight weeks."

~ Kirk Mote | Founder & CEO of Rescue Site Services

"I was encouraged to get this book by a close friend. I've been feeling like I need to write another book. However, I haven't been that excited about the task in front of me.
Now I am ready to go. This is not a sit-down read, and say that was a nice book. It is a get your pen and paper out and let's get to work, book. The author has laid out a simple step-by-step guide taking you from A to Z to get your book published and to market in 8 weeks.
I would recommend this book to any business owner wanting to write a book to get your message to the masses. Go make it happen!"

~ Mark Weisenburger | CEO of Weisenburger Marketing Group

"I'd like to thank Mario Fachini, my Marketing & Publishing Coach & Mentor. We've been acquainted for many years, but I've just recently hired him to collaborate on my book project.

He was actually the first person to show me how to do Video Testimonials & also helped me come up with my Wealth Coaching title. I don't think I would have been able to get this book done in eight weeks if it had not been for him & all his help, encouragement, understanding & prompting as well as keeping me accountable to push through & reach my goal.
I had been talking about writing a book (of my own) for years, Mario helped me make it a reality. I will be forever grateful to him for getting me started in my new path as a real bonafide (solo) author. He has helped me realize my new acronym in another way: M.A.N.O.L.A. ~ Making Another New Outstanding Life Achievement."

~ **Manola Webster** | Founder & CEO of Making Wealth Attainable

www.ingramcontent.com/pod-product-compliance
Lightning Source LLC
Chambersburg PA
CBHW031521120626
46545CB00005B/1934